COPING
WITH STRESS
IN COLLEGE

COPING WITH STRESS IN COLLEGE

MARK ROWH

College Entrance Examination Board, New York

In all of its book publishing activities the College Board endeavors to
present the works of authors who are well qualified to write with authority
on the subject at hand, and to present accurate and timely information.
However, the opinions, interpretations, and conclusions of the authors are
their own and do not necessarily represent those of the College Board;
nothing contained herein should be assumed to represent an official position
of the College Board, or any of its members.

Copies of this book are available from your local bookseller or may be
ordered from College Board Publications, Box 886, New York, New York
10101-0886.

Editorial inquiries concerning this book should be directed to Editorial
Office, The College Board, 45 Columbus Avenue, New York, New York
10023-6992.

This book is dedicated to my Mom and Dad, Coy and Evelyn Rowh, and to all parents who have helped a son or daughter fulfill their college dreams.

CONTENTS

Contents

*F*OREWORD

*G*raduating from college is an integral part of the American dream for millions of people. Going off to college (or commuting to a nearby institution) represents a major step in many young people's lives. This bold new venture is usually accompanied by great expectations on the part of students and their families, and often by great fears. After all, success in college is widely seen as a requirement for a worthwhile career, and a ticket to "the good life."

Not only is a lot riding on collegiate efforts, but the experience itself represents a major life change. For most students it includes a break from the lifestyle they have always known, and their first real venture into the world of adults.

These and other factors can cause a high degree of stress for college students. This stress can cause serious problems, or it can be managed so that students meet their various challenges without falling victim to undue stress. And that is the reason this book has been developed. Mark Rowh offers an overview of the problems stress can cause for college students, along with helpful tips on managing their new and challenging situation. Building on his own experience as a student, professor, and college administrator, he has developed a series of strategies any student can follow to make college life a less stressful experience.

The student who reads this book attentively will probably find far fewer disruptive surprises upon entering college than the student who is not familiar with this material. Mark Rowh does an excellent job of helping students anticipate the stressful aspects of attending college and identify their own areas of potential stress. The book includes chapters on positive and negative stress, taking stock of ones own situation, the pressures of meeting expectations, coping with emotional stress, time management, overcoming test anxiety, writing papers, handling the pressure of speaking before groups, the physical side of dealing with stress, and more. It offers a plethora of examples of how students deal both effectively and ineffectively with stress. From Rowh's examples and suggestions, a student can gain a clear idea of stressful situations to avoid; the specific kinds of support for which to look; concrete suggestions on improving study habits, note taking, efficient reading, and more.

In my own work at the University of Utah School of Medicine, I have seen some students respond to the stress of learning by feeling threatened and focusing on potential loss and helplessness, while other students feel challenged and focus on intellectual growth and hope. The difference between these types of students is that the successful student, among other things, is clearly informed as to what is expected and knows how to prepare for tests, papers, or presentations. Even if the student has little control over whether or not a stressful event occurs, taking charge—by asking what professors expect and appropriately preparing—will free him or her from a sense of helplessness. It will leave the student more excited about learning. Likewise, those entering college who take charge by following the suggestions in Mr. Rowh's book will certainly feel more of a sense of control and excitement about attending college because they will be better informed and prepared from having read this book.

David C. Spendlove
Assistant Professor
Department of Family and
Community Medicine
University of Utah School of Medicine

CHAPTER 1

*S*TUDENT STRESS

*I*f you're old enough to go to college, you've probably suffered countless lectures about how tough it's going to be. High school teachers, counselors, parents, and others have hammered this point home as often as possible. In fact, the mere mention of the word *college* is often used as a scare tactic.

Do any of these phrases sound familiar?

From that demanding English teacher: "You can't write like that and expect to get by in college."

From the math teacher who seems to believe everyone should be able to think in equations instead of normal language: "You think this is tough? Wait until you hit college."

Your *counselor:* "You've got to keep your grades up if you want to get into a good college."

Everybody's free advice, whether you ask for it or not: "If you want a good job, you need a college education."

Words of wisdom from all the leading authorities: "If you want to succeed in college, the College Board's *Coping with Stress in College* is a must" (OK, so we sneaked that one in on you!)

Your well-meaning *parent:* "I didn't get to go to college, but you're going even if we need to take out a second mortgage."

Another version of the *well-meaning parent:* "Your grandfather, your mother, and I all benefited from college. Of course you will carry on the family tradition."

From the "honest" *friend or relative:* "You, in college? You'll never make it."

Or from *any number of sources*, that clincher everyone wants to hear: "Go get 'em. You know we're all counting on you!"

Every student has to live with sentiments such as these. Long before you ever step foot on a college campus, subtle pressures—and those not so subtle—begin to influence you as you look ahead to that yawning chasm, *the future.* After all, you want to be happy, right? And to be happy, you must be successful. And the third part of the formula: you've got to get a good education. For several million Americans every year, this means embarking on the long, arduous, and often stressful experience of trying to make it in college.

Just thinking about it is enough to raise your blood pressure. Simply to get to college in the first place, you will need to surmount all kinds of barriers, from surviving the college admissions process to finding enough money to pay for it all. Consider the enormity of the questions that must be addressed.

Which college should I choose? Will I be admitted to my first choice? What if I'm turned down? Will I earn a scholarship or other financial aid? What will I major in? Should I go away to college or stay at home a little longer? These and other matters can press in on you from all sides as you try to make smart decisions and point yourself in the right educational direction.

And then once you actually begin your college career, the pressures really begin. First, you must adjust to the academic challenge of college-level work. At the same time, you'll be faced with all kinds of new social situations and other changes in your life. Suddenly your routine becomes vastly different from what it has been before, and you find yourself trying to adjust. The result? Regardless of the outcome, you are virtually certain to experience stress.

"Going to college is like crossing into a new culture," says Dr. Sharon Rubin, dean of the School of Liberal Arts at Salisbury State University in Maryland. "The disorientation and stress level are similar to what many people feel when they go to live in another country, away from everything and everyone supplying emotional and practical support. As a result, most college students face a high degree of stress."

Stress. That's a word you see and hear frequently. And it's the key concept behind this book. As a guide for managing the particular kinds of stress faced by college students, the book will cover all aspects of the subject in an effort to provide you with helpful information and workable strategies for coping.

Just what is stress? Ask several people, and you'll probably get as many answers. According to *The American Heritage Dictionary*, it is "a mentally or emotionally disruptive or disquieting influence; distress." For the purposes of this book, a somewhat broader definition applies. In the context used here, *stress* means any situation or state where a person experiences increased or anticipated demands, such as emotional demands, physical challenges, or both.

No matter who you are, you're certain to experience stress sometime. Women, men, business executives, grocery clerks, baseball players, movie stars, teachers, students—everyone faces stressful situations in their lives. In fact, it is estimated that nearly half the people in the United States suffer from some kind of stress-related problems during any given month. And over the long term, virtually everyone must deal with difficulties related to a high level of stress.

Although stress can affect anyone, college students and students preparing for college are particularly susceptible. Indeed, students as a whole represent one of the most stress-prone groups in American society. After all, where else can you find a lifetime of academic preparations put at risk, where one semester or even one course can lead to total failure and a complete change of life direction?

In a way, surviving college life can be compared to walking down the center line of a busy four-lane highway, with thousands of others following single file behind you. As long as you keep up a steady pace everything is fine, but if you lose your concentration you can drift aside, either falling by the wayside or perhaps even getting flattened by an 18-wheeler. In either case, you will end up just one individual casualty, while the line continues steadily on, oblivious to your predicament.

Sound scary? Actually, the real world of college life need not be so imposing. Nobody claims it will be easy, but on the other hand the road through college can be negotiated. Each year, according to the U.S. Department of Education, over 980,000 people earn bachelor's degrees from American colleges and universities, and more than 420,000 complete two-year, associate degrees. That's well over a million success stories every year! You can be one of them, but to help guarantee your success it will be important to recognize some of the main causes of stress in college students' lives and learn how to deal with them effectively.

Adapting to a New Environment

The very act of starting college is almost sure to be one of the most stressful changes in your life. You've already encountered similar situations, with transitions from elementary school to middle school or junior high, and then again to high school. Do you remember the strain of trying to fit in at a new school? Chances are you experienced a fair share of pressures and uncertainties while trying to cope with everything from being picked on by older students, to wondering why in the world anyone would care about obscure algebra problems involving something as silly as two trains traveling in opposite directions.

Or maybe your family moved to a new town at some point in the past, and you had to face the ritual of making new friends and developing an entirely new social routine, not to mention the academic challenges of a strange school.

Going away to college requires an even greater capacity for coping. The reason? For the first time, you will be completely on your own. In starting high school, you at least had the security of going home every day to the same environment. Even if it wasn't a perfect home headed by Mr. and Mrs. Cleaver or a father who always knew best, it still offered a degree of stability through its sameness. If a new school environment made all kinds of demands on your adaptability, you could always escape to the relative haven of home and family.

Tackling college, on the other hand, is a full-time proposition. Your new surroundings are not just a matter of classes and laboratories, but also the "after hours" world of dormitory or apartment living. From the time you wake up and on through every part of the day, you will be operating in a world that is completely separated from your previous everyday routine. This will mean everything from getting yourself up in the morning to setting your own schedule for doing homework, not to mention accommodating the needs of a roommate who may have very different ways of doing things.

At the same time, the academic environment will be unlike anything you have previously encountered. Your high school classes—or at least some of them—may have been difficult, but most college classes will be even more demanding. Many professors seem to thrive on deluging their students with work, cramming huge amounts of material into the space of one semester or academic quarter. They also tend to suffer from the "my class counts most" syndrome. Steeped in their own particular discipline, most faculty operate as though their classes are the only ones that really count. So what if you are overwhelmed with work for your other classes? To the typical professor, that is simply not relevant.

Not only is the volume of work heavy, but the depth of coverage is greater than in high school. A single course may cover a wide range of material, and students are expected to absorb more information. In a college psychology course, for example, you may be required to read a long, detailed textbook as well as several other books and articles. And the instructor's lectures may cover completely different topics, with students being expected to analyze and evaluate information instead of just memorizing facts they have been "spoon-fed" from a single source.

At any given time, you may find yourself struggling to complete reading assignments, write computer programs, conduct library research, do clinical or laboratory assignments, or prepare for exams. The combined load can be a source of real stress.

Test Anxiety

In addition to the stress brought on by change in your everyday routine, college lets you soar to new heights of pressure in other ways. Consider tests, for example. Go to college, and you will have to take tests. Lots of them. It's as inevitable as some of the other unpleasant but inescapable facts of life: death, taxes, or the sound of an alarm clock first thing in the morning.

The anxiety brought on by college exams can be worse than anything you've faced in high school. The material is more complex, the competition tougher, and in many classes the exams are less frequent, making each one that much more important in terms of its impact on your grade for the course. As a result, college exams can place tremendous levels of stress on you.

Handling test anxiety is an important skill, and one that you can acquire if you don't already possess it. Chapter 7 covers this in more detail.

Social Pressures

Stress is not caused by academics alone. For that to be true, grades would have to be about the only thing you consider important. But if you care what other people think of you, you are vulnerable to social pressures. Think of the potential stress involved in the following situations any college student might face:

—It's your first day on campus, and you stop in the college cafeteria for a quick lunch. There are only a few places left to sit, and the one you grab is in the midst of several students who already seem to know each other. You sit down and begin eating, awkwardly trying to avoid the appearance of intruding or listening in on their conversation. A couple of them glance up as you take your place, but then the conversation continues as if you're not even there. It's all very awkward, and the minutes seem to drag on like hours.

—It's party time! After a hard week of studying, you're enjoying the Friday night celebration sponsored by a local sorority. There's just one problem: first your date insisted you join in the drinking, even though you've never had much of a liking for alcohol. And then as the evening progresses and inhibitions break down, someone brings out the drugs. That would be bad enough, but your date starts pressuring you to join in. It seems as though whatever move you make will cause problems, and what had started out as an evening of fun has turned into a high-stress situation.

—The pile of books on your desk is imposing, and you sit there in your dorm room trying to go through each one so you'll be prepared for tomorrow's classes. But your roommate just won't let up! When he's not chattering about football or girls or what he's going to do tomorrow, he keeps playing the same two tapes of a rock group you don't particularly like. The result is constant distraction from your studies, not to mention a growing annoyance at his well-meaning but tiresome interruptions. So what do you do? Do you confront him and risk hurting his feelings or just silently bear it? Maybe you'll need to seek advice from the resident assistant. At any rate, the situation is not one you had expected, and it is growing into a major problem.

These are just a few examples of the kinds of situations college students face all the time. College life places you in the position of meeting new people, many of whom will have vastly different values and ways of doing things than you have previously experienced. The old social network of school friends and family will be replaced by new friends and new ways of spending your time, and in many cases this kind of change will be accompanied by high levels of stress. To make it in college, you must respond not just to academic pressures but to social ones as well.

Meeting Parents' Expectations

One reason college is stressful is that people expect so much of you when you take on the student's role. Especially parents. Remember the classical story about the young soldier who was told as he went off to battle to "return with your shield, or on it?" That wasn't some tough old sergeant who was admonishing the soldier about his duty. It was his mother!

In a way, parents tend to take the same kind of stance when they send their sons and daughters off to college. Sure, it's not really a life-and-death issue. But it's close! Many families are deeply serious about the whole issue of a college education for the children. Realizing this goal may require long-term planning and substantial sacrifices: many parents have saved for years or have taken out second mortgages or other loans that will take years to pay. Mothers have taken jobs with the specific purpose of paying college expenses for their children, and parents who are already employed have often been known to take second or even third jobs to come up with the thousands of dollars needed for a college education.

Even where finances are not a problem, parents often place more importance on the matter of college than on any other single consideration. In affluent families where success in college has become a tradition over several generations, graduating high school students face the task of measuring up to the records of previous family members. College is seen not so much as an opportunity for the newest generation, but as an obligation.

In either case, and in situations between the two extremes, the bottom line is that parents and other family members place great expectations on their children. When you take on the role of college student, you will probably be carrying along the hope and pride of those people who brought you into the world and helped you get this far. As you realize that your success is something others are counting on, the already substantial pressures involved in the collegiate experience can grow even greater.

Meeting Your Own Expectations

Of course parents are not the only ones with high expectations. Unless you were coerced into tackling college, the venture represents the key to your own goals and dreams for the future.

If you've been a good or excellent student in high school, part of your goals probably involve not just earning a college degree but doing well in the process. In fact, good students are often those who experience the most stress in college. They're the ones shooting for the A on every exam or aiming for the dean's list or trying to pile up an impressive grade-point average to gain later admission to law school, medical school, or some other graduate program. Good students tend to take the toughest courses, where not only is the subject matter imposing in itself, but the competition is often intense because the rest of the class is also made up of good students. As a result, the normal stresses of college life are compounded by self-imposed pressures.

If your academic record has not been that strong, your goals may be less ambitious but nevertheless just as important. Maybe you worry not about how well you will do in comparison to other students but simply whether you can make it in college at all. You want a good job and a challenging career, and the credentials provided by collegiate training are a necessary step along the way. College classes represent not some kind of game where you hope to impress people with your intelligence, but barriers that must be hurdled to reach job-oriented goals.

Whatever your past academic record, it can be pretty frightening to realize that you must start all over again. Accomplishments of the past will mean nothing once you begin your college career. And in planning for what you hope to make of your life, self-imposed pressures can add to the overall stress of college life.

The Demands of Constant Assessment

Some roles in our society are well known for the high levels of stress that accompany them. For example, consider the glamorous but pressure-filled job of a football coach at a major university. For two or three hours every fall Saturday afternoon, life becomes a rollercoaster of offense and defense, successful plays and those that never live up to the potential they showed on the drawing board, thunderous cheers and boos from the crowd, and seemingly limitless tidal waves of emotion.

Similarly, think of the stress that people must face in jobs that are physically dangerous. How anyone can have the nerve to defuse bombs or face down armed criminals is difficult to imagine for those who have never really faced danger.

The student's life may not include these kinds of hazards, but it has its own demands, including the pressure of constant assessment. Someone with a master's degree or a Ph.D. seems to be examining your every thought, looking for flaws or inaccuracies and eagerly pointing them out in whatever format is available. You turn in an essay in English 101 and get it back with corrections and criticisms scrawled all over the paper. As one of 150 students in a geography class, your only identity is a number and the scores you make on multiple choice exams. You stand in front of a public-speaking class, and not only the instructor but every student in the class weighs not just each word you speak but how you look. Every day, someone evaluates you or your work.

Living under constant scrutiny, dealing with test anxiety, adapting to a new environment, measuring up to the expectations of yourself and others—these and other pressure points can make college a difficult experience. But you can overcome these obstacles and more.

"Dealing with the challenges of college involves a lot of acquirable skills," Dr. Rubin says. "You will be thrust into an unfamiliar environment and asked to perform complex tasks with much less information and supervision than ever before. But you can step back from the experience you are in, analyze it and decide what to do next. And in developing this ability, you can learn to keep stress at a manageable level."

The remaining chapters of this book provide a variety of practical tips for coping with the stress anyone can encounter in college. By considering the various factors at work and applying creative strategies to your own particular needs, you can use this guide to deal effectively with college-related stress. You've made it this far, and you can do even better! And in the process, with the right approach, you can conquer stress instead of letting it get you down.

CHAPTER 2

*G*OOD STRESS, BAD STRESS

*T*he word *stress* usually carries negative connotations. "I'm stressed out" is a complaint voiced often by all kinds of people, college students included. And of course the whole point of this book is to help you control the negative side of stress. But like just about everything else in life, stress has more than one side to it. Certain kinds of stress actually exert a positive influence on your life, and it's important to understand the various aspects of this somewhat complicated concept.

Stress is more than the pressure you feel at exam time or the feeling of having more to do than can be accomplished. It also includes characteristics ranging from the emotional to the physical reactions a person makes to challenges or demands.

Fight or Flight

From the earliest times of primitive people, the human body has been programmed to respond when physically threatened. When confronted by a saber-toothed tiger or a tribe of strangely dressed humans (and remember, this was long before MTV!), early men and women became angry or fearful. Their bodies reacted accordingly, in what has been labeled the "fight or flight" syndrome. This is the body's propensity to react physically to the need for self-defense, either through confronting an enemy or running away.

Say you're alone late at night after just having suffered through the latest slasher movie, and then you hear a strange noise outside your window. You suck in your breath and strain to hear more sounds, images of screaming teens and bloody corpses fresh in your mind. It's probably nothing, you tell yourself, but nonetheless you are genuinely scared. So what happens? Your heart kicks into overdrive, and various muscles contract in anticipation of possible action. Your body readies itself for two alternatives: to fight or to run away. In either case, your body chemistry has changed, and the result is a higher level of readiness.

For a few moments you're ready to take on the world—or to make like a cartoon character zipping away from danger. But then you discover that the noise was only the wind blowing some shrubbery against the windowpane. As suddenly as the fright developed, the apparent danger dissipates. Gradually you begin to relax, and soon your body returns to its previous "normal" state.

In a less dramatic fashion, your body reacts to stress all the time. Stress factors come into play in everyday life in many ways. It's not just a matter of danger or fear, but also of other situations that may be far from life or death.

Take deadlines, for instance. When a professor assigns a paper, the task usually must be accomplished by a specified date. This in itself is not necessarily a problem, if the amount of time allotted is reasonable. You just complete the work on a gradual basis, and when the due date arrives you turn in the finished paper. But if you have a number of other competing assignments, it may be difficult to keep up with the schedule you had intended. You may begin to feel pressured by the volume of the work that must be accomplished, not only for this paper but in combination with everything else.

Or you may simply commit the common sin of procrastination, putting off work that can be completed later. Chances are this will eventually result in some definite unpleasantness, such as finding yourself working away at 3 a.m. the night before the paper is due. Your life might not be on the line, but an important grade is! And your body will let you know it doesn't appreciate the situation.

Does it have to be this way? No, but you will be vulnerable to this kind of stress unless you take steps to minimize the pressures. You cannot entirely avoid difficult assignments, but you *can* make things less strenuous by thinking your way through each situation. During class registration, for example, take some time to analyze the work load involved before signing up for too many difficult courses during the same term. And when a professor makes an assignment that obviously will take hours or days to complete, set up a schedule that will allow you to do the work over a reasonable period of time instead of waiting until the night before it is due.

More tips on limiting the stress that comes with academic work are provided in later chapters. The main point to remember, though, is that although some negative effects of stress are unavoidable, many problems can be avoided by your own preventive actions.

Stress Is Not a Four-Letter Word

Even though too much stress causes problems, it's smart to realize that *stress* is not necessarily a bad word. It does have its positive aspects. A world without the influences of stress would not be a very progressive one. Imagine where our society would be if everyone were totally laid back all the time. If nobody ever felt pressured, what incentive would there be to improve life?

Think about it. If Paul Revere and his buddies had not felt motivated to take action, we'd all probably be speaking with British accents on our way to the local cricket match. Without a high degree of pressure, you probably would never have learned everything you now know. Remember the third grade and the imposing task of memorizing your multiplication tables? Without the fear of failure and the pressure exerted by that teacher who was a lot bigger than you, you probably would not have mastered this seemingly useless information as quickly.

In fact, as noted physician and stress expert Hans Seyle points out in his book *Stress Without Distress*, the only way to eliminate stress completely is to die. Experiencing stress means your body is responding to different influences exerted on it. The only stress-free situation would be one with zero body functions. And since dying almost always ruins your chances to land a good job, getting rid of stress entirely does not seem a desirable option!

"Stress isn't something you should try to eliminate entirely," says John Krafka, assistant director of recreational services at Georgia State University in Atlanta. "Try to learn to manage stress, not avoid it. Stress will be with you all the time, so try to channel it into something good."

Be sure to understand that stress is not caused only by bad or negative circumstances. In a sense, your body doesn't know the difference between positive and negative. An unexpected change or a highly emotional experience can cause the same kind of physiological response as a problem or threat.

For instance, imagine yourself walking into a room and finding your best friend crying buckets of tears. What's wrong, you ask? Between sobs, she tells you that her dog—

the special beagle she's had since she was a toddler—has been killed by a car.

Now, consider the same scene, but with different circumstances. You enter the room to discover your friend crying, and you immediately wonder what happened. Was it something terrible? No, she squeezes out between sobs. She just won $10 million in the state lottery!

These two situations may be poles apart, but the physical manifestations are virtually the same. In both cases, an unexpected event crashed into your friend's world like a shock wave. And in both cases, extra stress was placed on the body as it tried to cope with a situation that had not been anticipated.

Whether stressful events or situations are "good" or "bad," they place extra demands on the body. But if the time span involved is relatively short, the overall effect is minimal. You will probably feel a little tired—a common reaction to an encounter with suddenly induced stress—but after the body rests and renews itself everything should return to normal.

Long-term stress, on the other hand, can have an entirely different character. For example, picture yourself struggling through a semester when everything has gone wrong. Your application for a loan fell through, and you've had to work at a fast food restaurant while juggling the usual array of freshman classes. Money always seems to be a problem, and if that's not enough you just found out you're flunking biology. Lately you've begun to have trouble sleeping, and about the only time you don't have a headache is when you're suffering from an upset stomach.

You may not realize it, but you're more than a victim of bad luck. You're also suffering from too much stress. The various pressures of your life have combined to assault your emotional and physical well-being, grinding down your defenses and opening the way for a range of discomforts—and even physical illness if these pressures are not brought under control.

Physical Problems

Physical manifestations of emotionally triggered situations can become chronic problems, stretching over a long period of time and diminishing your overall health and effectiveness. A major factor is the body's ability to produce certain chemicals during periods of stress. When the brain detects a threat, it initiates changes in the body the way the Air Force scrambles jet fighters if an unknown intruder appears on a radar screen. But instead of F-16s, the human body produces special chemicals designed to heighten senses and increase levels of strength and energy.

The main producer of these substances is the adrenal gland, which produces the hormones adrenaline and cortisol. When increased adrenaline is released into the bloodstream, it helps you run faster, hit harder, or do whatever is physically necessary to react to a short-term problem. Cortisol causes similar changes on a more long-term basis, with changes also being affected by other glands such as the thyroid and the pancreas.

In a tight spot, these hormones can enhance performance. Whether this means surviving a real-life fight or simply getting that extra burst of energy needed in a sports contest, the added capabilities spurred on by such bodily chemicals can make the difference in succeeding rather than failing. But if the body continues to produce high levels of stress-triggered hormones on a long-term basis, the end result can be serious problems such as ulcers, skin disorders, high blood pressure, heart attacks, or strokes.

In fact, researchers have found a direct link between stress and physical illness. If you are subjected to too much stress, some kind of undesirable physical change is almost sure to result.

The work of Thomas Holmes and Richard Rahe, two noted researchers, has revealed direct connections between significant changes in people's lives and physical illness. They found that major changes had definite health implications, and too much change within a short period of time was more than most people could handle.

Their now famous "Social Readjustment Rating Scale" rates major events that individuals can experience in terms of how much stress they cause. For example, this scale equates the death of a spouse as amounting to 100 points, divorce as 73 points, getting married as 50 points, and so on. At the other end of the scale, less traumatic events such as Christmas (13 points) or getting a traffic ticket (11 points) also cause stress. Although a single event can be handled, a combination of too many life changes within a short period is likely to lead to illness. The higher the point total, the more likely that stress-induced illness will occur (with a total of 150–300 points for changes in a given year, there is a 50-50 chance of a serious health problem occurring, and a 90 percent chance for scores over 300).

Specific changes and their stress ratings are shown in the chart below (which is reprinted by permission from the *Journal of Psychosomatic Research*, vol. 11, 1967.)

Event	**Stress Rating (points)**
Death of spouse	100
Divorce	73
Marital separation	65
Jail sentence	63
Death of close family member	63
Personal injury or illness	53
Marriage	50
Fired from job	47
Marital reconciliation	45
Retirement	45
Change in a family member's health	44
Pregnancy	40
Sex difficulties	39

Addition of family member 39
Business readjustment 39
Change in financial status 38
Close friend's death 37
Change to a new field of work 36
More/less husband/wife arguments 35
Mortgage over $10,000 31
Loan or mortgage foreclosure 30
Change in work responsibilities 29
Son or daughter leaving home 29
In-law troubles 29
Personal achievement 28
Wife starting/stopping work 26
Ending or beginning school 26
Change in living conditions 25
Major change in personal habits 24
Trouble with employer 23
Change in work conditions/hours 20
Change in residence 20
Change in schools 20
Change in recreation 19
Change in church activities 19
Change in social activities 18
Loan or mortgage under $10,000 17
Change in sleeping habits 16
Change in number of family
get-togethers 15
Change in eating habits 15
Vacation 13
Christmas 12
Violations of the law (minor) 11

As you can see, even vacation causes stress as your routine is upset (13 points), and an outstanding personal achievement will add some 28 points to your stress index.

When you consider that starting college may involve several of these factors (26 points for beginning school, 16 points for change in sleeping habits, 15 points for change in eating habits and more), the potential impact of stress on every student's life becomes evident. And when the unique stressors involved in each person's life are also included, the overall impact of beginning college and then reacting to the various resultant changes looms even larger.

Of course numbers such as these are just guidelines, but they do provide an overall picture of the effect various life events can have on your health. A college student who experiences a death in the family or the divorce of parents, for example, will certainly face high stress levels. And even without dramatic changes, the many academic and social pressures of college can combine with serious effect.

Whenever an individual encounters too much stress, especially over a long period, physical problems are almost certain to appear. Here are just some of the effects too much stress can cause in your body:

> *Headaches.* Muscular tension in your neck and shoulders is a common side effect of stress, often leading to that old malady, the splitting headache. Headaches may not be life threatening, but they can certainly make your life miserable. College-level work is difficult enough without having to endure headaches while trying to master it, and the noise of most dormitories can drive you to distraction if your head is pounding.

> *Skin problems.* The changes in body chemistry caused by stress can result in worrisome skin rashes, especially for those who have a tendency to develop skin problems due to allergies or other causes. This side effect of stress is not as widely recognized as some of the others, but it can certainly be a nuisance.

> *Ulcers.* Ulcers aren't just a problem encountered by older people. College students can develop ulcers too, and stress is a leading cause. Changes in body chemistry

and blood flow can throw the stomach out of kilter, resulting in painful and even incapacitating ulcers. Or the same factors can lead to indigestion, a less severe but still hardly desirable condition.

Diarrhea. Nobody likes to mention the "D word," but it happens! And stress is sometimes the cause. Aside from the physical discomfort, this can be a great source of inconvenience and embarrassment.

Lack of sleep. If you're losing the war against stress, one of the most common outgrowths is lack of sleep. Either you can't go to sleep without first laying awake for hours, or you sleep fitfully without really getting the depth of rest needed. This is a problem for anybody, but for students it's one of the most frustrating situations you can encounter. Who wants to be suffering through an 8 a.m. class when you can barely keep your eyes open, let alone absorb the material being covered? The hour seems to drag on forever, and worst of all you become a bystander to the learning process—a result that's likely to show up during the next exam!

Heart problems. If stress continues to alter the body's status over a long time, one of the most serious repercussions can be damage to your cardiovascular system. High blood pressure can result, and that in turn can lead to heart attacks, strokes, or other heart-related problems. Of course this is more likely to occur in older adults, but the behavior patterns you establish as a young adult can help you head off such problems later.

Breathing difficulties. Stress can also contribute to breathing problems, especially in people with a history of lung ailments. Stress can trigger asthma attacks, for instance, as well as aggravating other lung conditions. Such ailments are always tough to deal with, and they can have serious repercussions for anyone trying to keep up with the rapid pace of most college work.

Sweating. Cartoonists and movie producers seem to love scenes where characters sweat profusely when placed under stress. A secret agent strains to pick a lock just before the bad guys show up, with beads of sweat popping out on his forehead. In the movie "Broadcast News," an accomplished journalist perspires so badly that he blows his shot at anchoring the evening news. Even characters such as Charlie Brown and Garfield fall victim to this common stress-related problem. Excess sweating on campus may not be a crime, but it's one side effect of stress that most people would rather do without.

Backaches. Muscular tension brought on by stress often leads to backaches. Like headaches, they can be a real distraction to your studies and a source of frustration as well as pain. An additional problem with backaches is that once you get one, it can be hard to get rid of it. That can lead to lack of sleep and other problems, not to mention the discomfort of trying to sit in the uncomfortable student desks found in many classrooms.

Depression. Prolonged stress can lead to clinical depression, which is more serious than simply feeling "down" because you can't seem to get started on that research paper for freshman English, or simply because it's a beautiful weekend and you don't have anywhere to go. This more serious brand of depression can include such problems as feeling listless or bored, losing your appetite, feeling lonely, crying easily, having an overall sense of hopelessness, and even suicidal thoughts. It can be one of the more serious offshoots of undue stress.

Other problems. Stress can also lead to other physical problems including palpitations, blurred vision, and difficulty in swallowing. Some people also feel there is a link between stress and colds or flu. At any rate, there is no doubt that high levels of stress can contribute to a variety of physical problems. Different people react in different ways to similar stressors, but it is generally true that when you face stress over an extended period, your health is likely to suffer.

Emotional Fallout

When you think about it, the whole stress situation seems a continuous cycle. Emotional pressures lead to physical problems, and in turn physical problems erode emotional well-being. For example, say you have a tension headache, brought on by the stress of worrying about midsemester exams. Not only does the headache cause physical pain, but it keeps you from concentrating properly on the materials you are trying to absorb. That only makes matters worse from an emotional viewpoint, as you begin to get discouraged and desperate, feeling that your chances of doing well on your next exam are getting worse, not better. And of course this doesn't help your headache but can actually make it worse.

Or consider how stress can affect personal relationships. If stress causes you sleeping problems, for instance, you may become strung out and grumpy. This certainly won't endear you to friends or relatives, and it can put a real damper on your love life. Have you ever been in a grouchy mood and made a remark you immediately wished had stayed buried in the recesses of your brain, instead of being blurted out in anger or irritation? Once it's said, though, the damage is probably done, and you can't take back harsh words the way Detroit recalls defective cars. Everybody goofs sometimes, but those under stress are more likely to make such mistakes. You know how it is when you feel pressured: inhibitions break down, your patience is limited, and you don't necessarily stop and think before you act.

Stress often contributes to bad decisions. Have you ever wanted to pull your car out onto the highway, only to grow impatient as a stream of cars keeps coming from each direction? You sit there waiting for an opening, but the traffic just keeps coming, without a long enough gap to allow you to pull out safely. The seconds tick by, and your natural impatience is compounded as several cars line up behind you. So what do you do? After several minutes have passed and the tension grows, you suddenly punch the accelerator, whip out on the road, and force another driver to hit his brakes to avoid hitting you. The move wasn't really necessary, but you lost perspective and took a chance anyway.

In the life of a student, too much pressure can cause equally bad decisions. Too often, students drop a class halfway through the term when they might well survive it, but the stress of a big exam or paper deadline clouds their judgment. In an even further extreme, too many students react to the overall pressure of academic life by dropping out of school entirely. This is not necessarily a bad decision, for in some cases going to college in the first place turns out to be the wrong move. But too often, leaving college is an emotional decision reached during times of high stress, rather than a calmly rendered one made slowly and carefully.

Another extreme involves cheating. Some students fall into the trap of cheating out of desperation rather than laziness or innate dishonesty. Sure, some misguided souls use cheating as an easy way to avoid work, but sometimes otherwise honest students find the pressure too intense and resort to cheating when the opportunity presents itself. And of course that is always a mistake, whether or not the action is ever discovered. The old truism about "only cheating yourself" is right on target when it comes to college and the learning process.

Limiting the Negative

As you can see, stress is not something that can be eliminated, nor should it be. The key is taking advantage of the positive aspects of stress and learning to manage the negative.

If you're tackling an exam, for example, try to use the natural stress of the situation to your advantage rather than letting it control you. Just as many athletes perform better when the pressure is on, you can utilize the intensity of the test environment to help produce an enhanced performance. By "psyching yourself up" when the situation calls for it, you can increase your potential for success.

Similarly, use your own goals as tools to prod yourself into taking the necessary actions to succeed. The very act of enrolling in college represents a statement that you intend to do something with your life. But you won't make it unless you force yourself to do the work required. Nobody says studying for an exam or reading a difficult textbook is fun, and there will inevitably be times when you would rather do *anything* than the academic task at hand. But the alternative is failure. Fear of failure, as long as it is not an unreasonably dominating concern, can provide a useful degree of stress.

At the same time, too much stress will definitely cause problems. And dealing with it means more than just the latest health or exercise fad. Instead, managing stress is a vital and fundamental process. You will need to deal effectively with stress to make it in college, and the coping strategies you develop as a student will prove invaluable later in life. If you want good health as well as success, the ability to manage stress will be a necessity.

CHAPTER *3*

*Y*OUR STRESS
PROFILE

*O*ne of the nicest features about college life is the variety of backgrounds and lifestyles that students bring together. A student from a small mountain town in Tennessee might share a room with another from Boston, while down the hall a student from Nigeria rooms with another from rural South Dakota. In classrooms as well as dormitories, students and professors represent different economic levels, cultural backgrounds, religious beliefs, political views, and more.

A campus poll of what constitutes a good time would probably harvest a wide range of responses at most colleges. Where one student loves rock concerts, another might spend all his free time absorbing classical music and mastering the grand piano. For every gregarious soul who relishes parties or late-night discussion sessions and always prefers to be part of a crowd, there is probably another who prefers a quiet, orderly schedule and a couple of hours with a good novel. Some are early risers; others are night owls. One might find the pounding of rock music a necessary background for studying, lounging around, and virtually every other waking moment, whereas another may find the sound of a pin dropping a major distraction.

Just as nobody's lifestyle is identical to anyone else's, the same is true of individual personalities. Different people can face similar situations and yet react entirely differently. For example, the next time you're standing in line to buy tickets to a concert, study how the other people in line behave. Some will wait calmly, chatting with friends, reading or listening to headphones, or just passing time. Others will be tapping their feet nervously, becoming tense or showing signs of irritability as the waiting obviously takes its toll.

In fact, some people are just naturally more susceptible to stress than others. As shown on the NBC news special "Stressed to Kill," even babies have different reactions to stress, with some becoming more easily distressed under controlled situations than other infants. The same is true for children, adults, and college students.

Type A or Type B?

After conducting studies on how people react differently to stress, researchers Meyer Friedman and Roy H. Rosenman identified two basic types of personalities: Type A and Type B. Those in the first category tend to be more aggressive people who always seem energized. They also tend to be more susceptible to high blood pressure and other physical problems related to stress. Type B personalities, on the other hand, generally move at a slower pace. Instead of always being in a hurry or driving themselves to accomplish things,

Type B folks tend to be more laid back. And on the average, they develop fewer problems with blood pressure and other stress-related maladies.

It's interesting to think about your own personality and determine which type seems most like you. If you see yourself in any of the following, you may be a Type A personality:

—Your friend is relating the plot of the latest movie, but you can't wait until he is finished. Waiting for him to get to the final scene just makes you nervous, and if you could, you would reach over and pull the words right out of his mouth.

—There's a long line of people waiting to enroll for fall classes. Some people seem to be taking it in stride, but you find yourself becoming more and more irritated. In fact, the idle chatter of some of the other students is really getting on your nerves.

—You're one of those people who just can't sit still. You're always drumming with your fingers, pulling at your hands, tapping your feet, or shaking your knees. It's not something you think about or do consciously, but just a basic part of your personality.

—You always talk fast or make rapid gestures when talking, or both.

—You get upset if you lose a game of Monopoly, a "friendly" game of tennis, or some one-on-one basketball. For you, any sport or game means a chance to win, and winning is very important.

—It really bothers you to watch your little brother putting together a block house or to sit back and watch your sister assemble a jigsaw puzzle. You know you can do it better.

—You constantly find yourself thinking about grades, points scored or anticipated in ball games, sales quotas for Junior Achievement, or other tangible measures of accomplishment.

OK, so what if you are a Type A? Is that entirely bad? Not necessarily, for many of the more aggressive attributes typical of Type A personalities can help you get ahead in life. If you could administer an exam testing for this factor to famous athletes, movie stars, political leaders, or other prominent, successful people, chances are many would demonstrate a substantial share of Type A characteristics. Similarly, some of the more relaxed qualities of Type B personalities might be good for physical health but actually turn out to be an impediment in terms of motivation to succeed or excel in academics, career advancement, or other important areas.

Still, the link between Type A behaviors and heart disease seems significant enough to warrant special attention. If you fit under this grouping, it would be wise to develop coping strategies so that you can change at least some of your behavior patterns, ward off avoidable stress, and improve your prospects for good health.

For example, try "forcing" yourself to relax at several preset intervals during each day instead of crashing headlong through your schedule like a bull in a stockbroker's commercial. If you're strongly Type A, this may seem strange at first, but after you get used to it you may find yourself looking forward to these brief respites, even if they last only five minutes each. Try just doing nothing for these few minutes, brushing aside any substantive thoughts about tasks or worries. Or use a specific relaxation technique such as deep breathing or visualization (covered in more detail in chapter 11).

If you are prone to frequent bouts of anger, develop a system for calming yourself down before the emotion takes complete control of your body. Remember the old advice about counting to 10 before reacting to some source of frustration? Such a strategy *can* work, although for some people it may be more effective to pause for a longer period or use some other diversion. Another approach is to use physical activity. Taking a brisk walk or using an exercise machine, for instance, can help replace anger with a feeling of calmness.

A Self-Test for Stress

To help you take a closer look at your own stress situation, here are some questions you can ask yourself. By rating your various responses, you can arrive at a perceived stress score. Don't worry about the results; just approach this exercise in a spirit of fun to clarify some points about your own behavior.

The following scale, developed by Dr. Sheldon Cohen at Carnegie Mellon University, poses questions about your thoughts and feelings during the last month. For each question, you will respond *how often* you thought or felt a certain way. Although some questions seem similar, each is unique and you should deal with each one as a separate question. The best approach is to answer fairly quickly—don't attempt to count the number of times you felt a particular way, but indicate instead the alternative that seems a reasonable estimate.

For each question, choose from the following alternatives:

Never
Almost never
Sometimes
Fairly often
Very often

1. In the last month, how often have you been upset because of something that happened unexpectedly?

_____ never (0 points)
_____ almost never (1 point)
_____ sometimes (2 points)
_____ fairly often (3 points)
_____ very often (4 points)

2. In the last month, how often have you felt that you were unable to control the important things in your life?

_____ never   (0 points)

_____ almost never   (1 point)

_____ sometimes   (2 points)

_____ fairly often   (3 points)

_____ very often   (4 points)

3. In the last month, how often have you felt nervous and "stressed"?

_____ never   (0 points)

_____ almost never   (1 point)

_____ sometimes   (2 points)

_____ fairly often   (3 points)

_____ very often   (4 points)

4. In the last month, how often have you dealt success-fully with day-to-day problems and annoyances?

_____ never   (4 points)

_____ almost never   (3 points)

_____ sometimes   (2 points)

_____ fairly often   (1 point)

_____ very often   (0 points)

5. In the last month, how often have you felt that you were effectively coping with important changes that were occurring in your life?

_____ never   (4 points)

_____ almost never   (3 points)

_____ sometimes   (2 points)

_____ fairly often   (1 point)

_____ very often   (0 points)

6. In the last month, how often have you felt confident about your ability to handle your personal problems?

_____ never   (4 points)

_____ almost never   (3 points)

_____ sometimes   (2 points)

_____ fairly often   (1 point)

_____ very often   (0 points)

7. In the last month, how often have you felt things were going your way?

_____ never   (4 points)

_____ almost never   (3 points)

_____ sometimes   (2 points)

_____ fairly often   (1 point)

_____ very often   (0 points)

8. In the last month, how often have you found that you could not cope with all the things you had to do?

_____ never   (0 points)

_____ almost never   (1 points)

_____ sometimes   (2 points)

_____ fairly often   (3 point)

_____ very often   (4 points)

9. In the last month, how often have you been able to control irritations in your life?

_____ never   (4 points)

_____ almost never   (3 points)

_____ sometimes   (2 points)

_____ fairly often   (1 point)

_____ very often   (0 points)

10. In the last month, how often have you felt that you were on top of things?

_____ never   (4 points)

_____ almost never   (3 points)

_____ sometimes   (2 points)

_____ fairly often   (1 point)

_____ very often   (0 points)

11. In the last month, how often have you been angered because of things that happened that were outside of your control?

_____ never   (0 points)

_____ almost never   (1 points)

_____ sometimes   (2 points)

_____ fairly often   (3 point)

_____ very often   (4 points)

12. In the last month, how often have you found yourself thinking about things that you have to accomplish?

_____ never   (0 points)

_____ almost never   (1 points)

_____ sometimes   (2 points)

_____ fairly often   (3 point)

_____ very often   (4 points)

13. In the last month, how often have you been able to control the way you spend your time?

_____ never   (4 points)

_____ almost never   (3 points)

_____ sometimes   (2 points)

_____ fairly often   (1 point)

_____ very often   (0 points)

14. In the last month, how often have you felt difficulties were piling up so high that you could not overcome them?

_____ never   (0 points)

_____ almost never   (1 points)

_____ sometimes   (2 points)

_____ fairly often   (3 point)

_____ very often   (4 points)

Before scoring, make certain that you have marked each item separately. To score this self-test, write the number of points in the appropriate blank within each statement (important: notice that the order of point totals is not the same in each question; a response of "never" will earn 4 points in some questions and 0 points in others). Then add up your total score.

Your total will range somewhere between 0 and 56 points. The higher the point total, the higher your stress rating. A score between 15 and 20 total points might be considered average; between 20 and 30 moderately high; and above 30 high. A high score doesn't necessarily make you a basket case or an immediate candidate for a heart attack, and a low score doesn't mean you should just ignore the stress factors in your life. These scores are based on your perceptions, and scores could vary widely depending on your memory of the last month, the mood you're in when you answer the questions, and other factors. But your score can provide one yardstick to consider as you address your own particular program of stress-management strategies.

CHAPTER 4

*T*HE PRESSURES OF EXPECTATIONS

*W*hy do you want to go to college? Is it your own private dream, something that matters deeply to you, or is it more the fulfillment of someone else's expectations?

For Rick, a bright student with a penchant for building things and taking them apart, the chance to go to college represents an opportunity to become something no one else in his family has ever been: a professional in a highly paid, prestigious field. Rick's cousin attended a community college for a year and then dropped out to take a sales job, but no other family member has ever gone to college. Rick, on the other hand, wants to become an engineer. This has caused great excitement in his parents and other relatives, who constantly brag about their "future engineer" as they smile with obvious pride.

Rick's father and mother—a factory worker and a drug-store clerk—have not been able to save much money for tuition or other expenses, but they have taken out a second mortgage on their small house. With those funds, plus a scholarship, a student loan, and any money he can pick up from summer and part-time jobs, Rick should be able to scrape by.

Finances are not a problem in Leslie's family, where four generations before her have earned at least a bachelor's degree and several have been doctors, lawyers, and other professionals. Nor has there ever been a question of whether she would attend college. From as far back as she can remember, Leslie and all her relatives have assumed that her future would include higher education. The only real questions have been which "name" college she would attend and what professional field she would follow.

Unfortunately, Leslie has not turned out to be an outstanding student, unlike her older sister who was always garnering academic awards and the attention that went with them. Leslie's grades have been above average, but nothing to brag about. She knows she can never measure up to her sister's record, and sometimes she worries whether she will even make it in college at all.

No one has urged Mario to go to college. Instead, his father keeps nagging him to stay at home and help operate the family restaurant. "I need you," he keeps saying. "How will I manage without you?" Mario has worked in the restaurant part-time and summers, but he found the environment stifling. Instead, he would much rather pursue his dream of becoming a teacher. The one nearby college, though, does not offer a teacher education program, so there is no chance of commuting to school and helping out in the restaurant at the same time. Without room for compromise, Mario will need to go away to school, and the move will be made without the moral support of his parents.

Ginny doesn't have either support or resistance as far as college goes. Her parents divorced when she was only eight, and she hasn't seen her father for months. Her mother works two jobs and seems to have little time for her daughter. Ginny has tried to talk to her mother about college, but the conversations have always ended up touching on half a dozen other subjects without ever resolving anything about educational plans. It has become apparent to Ginny that her mother will not oppose her plans to go to college, where she would like to major in literature. But at the same time she will not be able to count on any support from home, financial or otherwise.

All these students have something in common. They are the target of extremely high expectations.

"There are almost always high levels of expectations involved in going to college," says Nancy Slater, director of counseling services at Columbia College in Missouri. "Some will come from yourself, and some will come from others. Trying to live up to these expectations can be extremely stressful."

Whether that pressure builds primarily from within or from others, the end result is the same. Going to college means putting a great deal on the line, and the need to meet certain expectations of this venture can generate a substantial level of stress.

Living Up to Parents' Expectations

Like it or not, you are an extension of your parents. Unless you come from a background such as Ginny's where nobody really cares what you do with your future, a reality of going to college is that you're representing more than yourself. You are also carrying on your back the hopes, plans, and dreams of your mother, father, or both. In fact you may even have more than two parents who feel they have a part in your success or failure, given the increasingly common touch of divorce and remarriage on today's families.

Just the sheer expense of a college education can bring significant pressure. College costs have shot out of sight in recent years, with the more prestigious colleges charging as much as $20,000 a year, and even those in a more moderate range such as state-supported universities costing several thousand dollars annually. Many families must struggle to come up with this kind of money, and when parents make financial sacrifices it places an added burden on the beneficiary of this generosity. This is not to say that parents will necessarily hold the money issue over your head, but if you love your folks, knowing they are making such an investment can't help but create some pressure for you to do well.

Finances aside, most parents want you to do an outstanding job in college. They can't help this; it's in their nature. The same pride that drives parents to cheer wildly at Little League baseball games, or follow every step at dance recitals or school plays, kicks in when you take the big step of enrolling in college. Whether you are the first person in your family to go on past high school or just one of many, the expectations of others will probably go along with you. In terms of stress, this can be a mixed blessing, providing incentive but also forcing you into a situation where success becomes even more important than might otherwise be the case.

Even when they mean well, parents can turn out to be problems in themselves. "Parents often push too much, and that can be difficult to deal with," notes Dr. Robert Stokes, director of continuing education and a former career planning director at Villanova University in Philadelphia. "They tend to make certain plans, and then expect their children to live up to them. I talked with one student, for example, who wanted to change majors but said he couldn't do it because his parents expected him to major in computer science."

Of course, most parents are not this directive, but those at the other end of the spectrum contribute to stress in a different way, according to Stokes. "A lack of support from parents can be just as bad," he says. "Maybe they just don't view college as important, or maybe they have other plans.

Some students have to fight tooth and nail simply to go in the first place, and then it's a continuing battle to stay in college until graduation."

Meeting Your Own Expectations

When you think ahead to your life as a college student, what kind of mental image develops? Maybe you picture yourself strolling down a shaded sidewalk after class, at least one attractive member of the opposite sex at your side. Or perhaps you're hanging out at the student center with a group of laughing, high-spirited friends. Of course, your grades are solid, and you are well regarded by professors and students alike. Not only are you popular, but others see you as someone on the move, a person who is confident and on target to success.

This is all well and good, but such expectations can be tough to turn into reality. If your actual college life ends up being less glamorous, the result may include not only disappointment but also the strain of struggling to measure up to your preconceived notions.

For many students, dreams for the future rest not so much on social considerations as the desire to make it in a certain career area. In such cases it is not simply a matter of succeeding in college, but succeeding in that specific academic field.

For example, maybe you have always wanted to become a nurse. As a small child, you asked for toy nurse kits for your birthday and played the role by bandaging up dolls, dogs, and anything else in sight. In high school you told everyone that your ambition was to be a registered nurse, and there is even a photo of you in the yearbook with a caption that includes "future R.N." beside your name. All the people in your life— teachers, relatives, friends—seem to know about these plans, and once you start college they tend to mention your studies whenever you run into them.

41

But in college your problems begin. You find yourself enrolled in several tough nursing classes, along with a couple of others such as English and psychology. There is a nutrition class that's a real killer, with an instructor who seems to take pride in the high failure rate in her classes. Worst of all is the clinical portion of the nursing classes, where your first experiences of actually working in a hospital include the constant feeling that someone is looking over your shoulder, just waiting for you to make a mistake.

The result: the normal level of stress is greatly increased as you strive to keep up with the heavy, difficult work load plus your own and others' expectations.

Reducing the Stress of High Expectations

So what do you do to reduce stress problems related to high expectations? The simplest advice would just be "don't worry about it." But life is rarely that simple. Instead, specific efforts on your part will probably be in order.

One way to limit the expectations of others is to reduce their personal investment in your success, whether that investment is tangible or emotional. For instance, if you can shoulder more of the financial burden, the investment becomes as much yours as anyone else's.

When I was an undergraduate, I was lucky enough to land a couple of scholarships that covered all my tuition and fees, plus books and other incidentals. By commuting to college and working part-time, I was able to cover 100 percent of college costs, including transportation. My parents were perfectly willing to sacrifice whatever was needed to support my college education, but as things turned out they didn't have to. In the process I felt an added degree of freedom, and at the same time faced very little stress based on anyone else's expectations. Everything felt like my own ball game. It seemed fine to major in English, a field I loved but which had limited career potential at the time. If my parents had gone into debt to bankroll my education, I might have felt compelled to major in something more "practical."

Covering all your own costs may not be possible, but taking out loans in your own name instead of your parents', earning scholarships or grants, and working summers or part-time all provide a measure of this kind of independence.

In other areas, it's often just a matter of defining and clarifying expectations. For example, say you have been an "A" student in high school. Do you expect to maintain an A average once you make the transition to college? If so, you're setting yourself up for some pretty high goals. That's commendable, but what if you don't make your objective? Rather than *expecting* to keep up an A average, perhaps you should set that as a goal, but at the same time make a deal with yourself that allows you some flexibility in terms of your real expectations. Be willing to settle for B's if necessary, and try to measure your success by standards that are not so arbitrary as a specific grade-point average.

In the same spirit, talk things over with anyone else who might have a stake in your education. If your father is big on grades, let him know you will do your best, but that he's not necessarily to expect your college record to match what you have accomplished in high school. Or if your mother has always dreamed of your going to law school but you're not really interested in a legal career, take time to talk things over before you get too involved in courses that are wrong for you.

For such discussions to have the best chance of success, do some homework ahead of time. For instance, instead of simply saying you'd rather not major in a given field, develop an alternative plan. Choose another area in which you are interested, and gather some information about the courses required, the job outlook, and other details that show you're serious about the matter. The better informed and more confident you appear, the more likely others are to accept your role in planning your own future.

Developing Contingency Plans

Everyone needs goals, and good planning is essential. But a part of this process is understanding that plans have a way of going awry. When things don't turn out as you had hoped, it's easy to become frustrated.

To lessen the potential for such frustrations to get you down, include some contingency plans with any projects or activities you undertake. For example, what would you do if you were finishing an important paper the night before it was due, and your typewriter or computer broke down? You could throw up your hands in desperation, or you could run around in a panic waking up friends and trying to borrow equipment. But if you had planned for the possibility of such a problem, it would not be as stressful. This planning could include an "emergency" arrangement with another student who has the same brand of typewriter or word processing equipment, to the effect that either of you could call on the other at any time, day or night, in an emergency situation.

A simpler contingency would be to set your own internal deadline which is two days before the actual due date announced by the professor. By establishing this "fudge factor," and making yourself stick to it, you would provide a safe period for taking care of unexpected problems. Instead of turning into a basket case, you could approach the situation in a calm and relatively stress-free manner.

Similarly, it's smart to prepare for other possibilities. A little contingency planning will go a long way toward preventing crisis situations. Some examples of such planning include:

- Stick a few dollars away in case you run short of funds unexpectedly.
- Save class "cuts" until you really need them because of illness or other emergency situations.

- Make certain you know the official last date when you may drop a class without an academic penalty (such deadlines are normally published in the catalog or schedule of classes).

- Always arrive for classes at least 10 minutes early. That way, you have an automatic grace period to offset last-minute delays.

- If you don't live on campus or within walking distance, develop an alternative plan to follow in the event your normal sources of transportation become unavailable. Get a bus schedule and keep it on hand, or find another student who commutes from the same area who would be amenable to taking on an occasional rider.

- When registering for classes each term, identify alternative classes that will meet the particular requirements of your program if any of your first choices are closed due to high enrollment or canceled because of insufficient interest. Thinking along these lines can prevent you from rushing into ill-considered choices.

- Arrange for at least one person in each of your classes to "cover" for you by sharing notes if you miss class. Even better, having two such contacts can help avoid problems if one happens to be absent the same day as you.

- Keep a travel clock in your room as a backup in case a power outage during the night renders your usual alarm clock ineffective.

Keep a balanced perspective as well. In considering various possible situations, try to preempt worries about failure by carefully considering exactly what failure really means. If you're having trouble with a class and worrying about receiving an F, ask yourself what the worst possible result would be if you actually failed. Will it mean flunking out of school? Probably not, unless you're also having similar difficulty in a number of other courses. Instead, it might mean repeating the course—not a particularly desirable option, but not the end of the world either. The same goes for many other points about which students worry. If you think it through, more often than not you will realize that your options are not all that limited.

CHAPTER 5

*C*OPING WITH EMOTIONAL STRESS

*T*here you are, sitting alone at your desk at 3 a.m., cramming for an exam that looms over you like an impending execution. Your eyes feel as though they are filled with sand; your back aches; and inside there is a feeling of mounting desperation as you find yourself losing in the race to absorb what seems an infinite amount of information.

Or picture yourself on a beautiful Saturday afternoon during your first month on campus. The day is gorgeous and you have some free time, but it might as well be just another school day as far as you're concerned. You've tried to make friends, but every encounter has left you tongue-tied or ignored, and you're beginning to wonder if you will ever find yourself anywhere but on the outside looking in. So here you are sitting on a bench with a textbook on your lap, looking up occasionally as other students stroll by in pairs and small groups, apparently unaware that you even exist. College may be fun for them, but for you it's a different story.

Do you worry about such possibilities? After all, going to college is certainly in your best interest, but that doesn't necessarily mean it will be easy. In fact, adjusting to college life can be one of the hardest tasks of your life. Chances are you'll be on your own for the first time, trying to fit into a strange environment where you're just one face in a crowd of strangers.

"Most students feel really nervous when they start out in college," says Kyle Morgan, an academic adviser at Ohio State University's Newark campus. "After all, everyone has heard plenty of horror stories about how hard it can be. And even on a small campus, you may feel like a number instead of a person as you enroll for classes and begin your studies."

Adjusting to Your New Independence

From the very first day of class, you will face the challenge of adjusting to a new, independent lifestyle. Suddenly you will be faced with all kinds of decisions. Would you benefit more from taking sociology or economics? Which English class will be your better choice—one at 8 a.m., when you can get off to an early start, or an early afternoon class, when you will be more fully awake? How heavy a course load should you attempt? Where should you eat lunch? Should you introduce yourself to that cute sophomore standing in line beside you at the bookstore?

At the same time, you will need to establish some kind of personal schedule and then learn to follow it. The days of Mom or Dad rousting you out of bed in the morning are gone, perhaps forever. Instead, you'll have to get yourself up on time every day, not to mention taking care of basic items such as your meals and laundry.

The reality of the situation is that for many students, college represents the first opportunity to operate on an adult level. You may have been allowed to flirt with adulthood before in such matters as learning to drive, attending adult movies, or perhaps voting, but in the educational setting the system has generally treated you as a child. Even in high school people were always making decisions for you and generally telling you what to do and when to do it.

The main mode of operation at the postsecondary level, on the other hand, is to leave you alone and let you manage your own affairs. Sure, there are rules, but nobody is going to look over your shoulder to see that every move you make is in your own best interest. Want to sleep in and skip that boring history class? Nobody will come after you, and your parents won't receive a telephone call that you've been cutting classes. Want to eat nachos for dinner every night? No one will remind you that you're not getting a balanced diet. Think a lighter course load will be easier to handle next term? It's your choice, even though the move will probably mean going to summer school or stretching out your studies for an extra semester or more.

So what does all this mean for you? In the first place, you will need to accept this new level of independence and become comfortable with it. For most students, the prospect of running their own lives sounds great, but there is a flip side to freedom. The flexibility to make more of your own decisions also brings the responsibility to make good ones. Otherwise, college can become a nightmare instead of an opportunity.

The Three C's of College Survival

In adjusting to the independent lifestyle of a college student, keep in mind three important concepts—consequences, change, and cooperation.

Consequences

Every decision you make will have certain *consequences*. If you decide to go to a basketball game instead of studying for the next day's physics exam, you will not be as well prepared for the test as would otherwise be the case. If you buy a pair of jeans and a couple of tapes, you may not have enough money to pay for that optional field trip sponsored by the art club. Choosing an English instructor with a reputation as an easy mark who gives everyone A's and B's might be good for your grade-point average, but it could prove damaging in other courses if your writing skills aren't improved.

A list of such decisions could go on almost endlessly. Most of them are not of the life-and-death variety, but they still matter, and as a college student you will find yourself making these kinds of decisions every day. Just remember that even though the choices may be up to you, the results aren't always as easily controlled. Whenever you find yourself facing a decision, be sure to think it through. Consider the consequences before you go ahead, and your new independence should be manageable.

Change

Never overlook the key fact that things *change*. If you are unhappy at first with your life as a college student, don't give up. As one day blends into the next, some of the hard new edges of your unfamiliar collegiate environment will begin to rub off. You will begin to make new friends, learn new routines, and eventually feel a part of things. The demands of academic performance will remain, but as you learn new things and improve your skills as a student, that should become less of a problem too.

In addition, the college calendar works to your advantage. Unlike high school classes, most of which extend over the entire academic year, college classes last only for one semester or quarter of anywhere from 12 to 16 weeks. So if you're having a miserable time in any particular class, it's nice to know that the experience will end in a matter of weeks, and you can look forward to a new set of classes and different instructors at the beginning of the next term.

A key point is that many changes are under your own control. If you planned to major in accounting but find out you hate the subject, you can switch to another major. If your roommate is driving you crazy, you can ask to be switched to another room or dorm. If the college you attend fails to measure up to your expectations, there's always the option of transferring to another school. Life might not ever be perfect, but the ability to change things provides a great opportunity to cope with factors causing too much stress.

Cooperation

A third element in making the most of increased independence is taking advantage of the *cooperation* that can be found whenever you need advice or help. Some of the nicest people you will ever meet are those who have selected college teaching, counseling, or a related job as their career. Such individuals tend to like people, and as a result they can be tremendous assets to students who are having problems or simply need information.

Of course, everyone you encounter will not be friendly or helpful, but every campus has enough of these student-oriented folks to go around. Whatever college or university you attend, you will find faculty, administrative staff, counselors, and other students who will take the time to talk with you and help you deal with the demands of college life.

Key contact persons include the the chief student affairs officer, who might be called the Dean of Students, Dean of Student Affairs, Vice President for Student Services, or some similar title, and who can point you in the right direction whenever you need help; your academic adviser; counselors, who might be located in a counseling center, attached to academic departments, or otherwise made available to students; the Director of Financial Aid or financial aid counselors, who can help if money is a problem; department chairpersons or deans in your area of interest; and faculty members, especially those instructors in your major area (for a listing of which persons to consult for specific types of help, see the chart provided later in this chapter).

Although you may feel isolated at times, remember that as a college student, you will not be alone. All around you will be people whose cooperation can help make the collegiate experience less stressful.

Dealing with Homesickness

The independence of college life is not only a matter of the practicalities of scheduling, meals, and so forth. It can also bring problems related to being separated from home and family. Homesickness is not just something encountered by young children when they go away to camp for the first time. It can be a very real problem for people of all ages, particularly young adults who suddenly find themselves separated from people who have been a close part of their life for as long as they can remember.

"Homesickness is one of the most common problems college students face," says Larry David, vice president of College Survival, Inc., a firm specializing in programs to help students succeed in college. "When you go off to college that usually means leaving others behind, and the separation can be very stressful."

Most of us have special relationships with certain people. You might be unusually close to your mother. Another student has been virtually inseparable from her younger sister. Still others relate especially well to a father, a special friend, a household of brothers and sisters, or a boyfriend or girlfriend.

It's understandable, then, for students to develop feelings of homesickness. When your environment has changed totally and the special people in your life are no longer a part of your everyday existence, you can find yourself feeling lonely and isolated, yearning for the familiar faces of home.

Fortunately, homesickness is not a fatal illness. In fact, it tends to subside as time passes even if you take no special measures, as you slowly adjust to your new setting and make new acquaintances. You can speed up the process, though, by making a concerted effort to deal with it.

Getting Involved in Student Activities

Probably the most effective method of fighting off this problem is getting involved and staying busy. If you have nothing to do but go to class and complete homework assignments, you are setting yourself up for boring evenings or weekends where there is little to do except mope around and think about home. But if you join one or several campus organizations and participate in their social activities, you will make new friends, the time will pass more quickly, and you will tend to dwell less on thoughts that lead to homesickness.

"Getting involved with some of the activities on your campus is a great way to beat homesickness," notes David. "This will provide a chance to meet new people and keep you from missing home so much."

Every college offers a variety of nonclass activities, such as student government, special interest clubs (for people with common interests in computers, music, creative writing, French, and so on), fraternities, sororities, newspaper staff, dramatic productions, religious clubs, and other organizations. Northern Kentucky University, for example, has more than 80 student organizations registered through its Office of Student Activities including the following:

American Advertising Federation

Anthropology Club

Art Council

Computer Science Club

Coalition of Sociology Students

Literature and Language Club

Pershing Rifles Club

Student Nurses Association

Black United Students

College Republicans

Young Democrats

Ski Club

Christian Student Fellowship '

Yearbook Club

Other institutions large and small sponsor various student organizations, each with its own special focus of interest. Participating in one or more will help balance your social life and make the transition to college a little less traumatic.

Staying in Touch with Those at Home

Another strategy is to keep in close touch with family and friends so you don't feel left out of what's going on at home. A hundred years ago going away to school usually meant a virtual break in contact except for an occasional letter, if that. But today, with telephones, relatively fast mail service, and various kinds of transportation available for making visits back home, you can keep in close touch even if you're hundreds of miles away. Just take the time to write or call on a regular basis, and you can develop a pattern of communication that will help ward off the blues.

If you get in the habit of sending frequent notes or postcards rather than long letters, you'll be more likely to keep up the flow of correspondence, which in turn should bring responses. And with inexpensive long-distance rates on weekends, you can use the telephone to stay close to friends or family without breaking your budget.

Making New Friends

For some people, making new friends is an easy, painless process. You know the type: they can walk into a room of strangers and feel perfectly at ease. In five minutes you would never know which person in the group was the newcomer.

For others, though, things may not be that simple. "The process of making new friends is often very stressful," notes Columbia (Missouri) College's Nancy Slater. "Many students have to work at this, and it's not always easy."

Whichever type you identify with, keep in mind that developing new friendships is an important step in adjusting to college life. There is no magic formula for making friends. Much of this depends on your own unique personality and how other people perceive you. But anyone can profit by using the following simple strategies to help the process along:

1. *Put yourself in a position to meet people.* You can't make friends if you stay in your dorm room all the time and otherwise keep a low profile. Whenever possible, take advantage of the chance to spend time with other students in informal situations where there will be a chance to talk and get to know them. Joining organizations is not the only avenue for this; you can make friends at ball games, concerts, the library, or even the laundromat. Even showing up a few minutes early to class can provide a chance to get to know other students.

Whatever else you do, avoid the habit of eating alone. Meals provide one of the best possible settings for informal conversation. Not only are meals more enjoyable when shared, but the process of eating itself keeps people partially occupied and thus helps lessen the perceived pressure to keep a conversation alive without interruption.

If you aren't already with friends, be sure to sit close to other people instead of going off alone. You can always join in a conversation about the quality of the food, if nothing else.

And once you begin talking, it should not be difficult to bridge to other subjects.

2. *Take the initiative.* If you wait for people to approach you first, you may miss out on a number of opportunities to develop friendships. When possible, grab the initiative by saying a few words to start a conversation. This is almost a "no lose" proposition. At worst, the other person just won't be very talkative, but at best one thing might lead to another and you could have a new friend before you know it.

If you're not sure what to talk about, just bring up something of common interest. Last night's rock concert, an upcoming exam, the latest movie in town, or the rumors about how tough the new political science professor is all represent good starting points, along with almost any other subject that fits the setting, such as how much you hate to wash clothes or how well the football team is doing.

3. *Give others the chance to talk.* It's great to start a conversation, but don't dominate it. I can remember standing in line at registration and overhearing a conversation that was really a monologue. One freshman introduced herself to another student and began telling her life story to him. She did all the talking except for his occasional brief responses, and it was obvious that he was not really enjoying the conversation. She was trying very hard—probably too hard—to make a friend, but it was not working.

A fundamental feature of human nature is that most people like to talk about themselves. Excellent conversationalists almost always do more listening than talking, realizing that giving people a chance to talk (especially about themselves or their particular opinions) makes them feel good. When you're chatting with another student, try to ask that person's opinion or to elicit talk about himself or herself. The result will probably be a more open response to your efforts to build a friendship, as well as providing you with a better idea of the other person's basic personality.

4. *Give it some time.* Friendships don't just blossom instantly; they take time to grow. Once you meet someone who

seems a potential friend, don't try to rush things. After all, as students you will be seeing each other frequently in attending class together or participating in common activities. If you are compatible, the friendship will develop naturally as you spend more time together. Trying to force the issue may make you seem too aggressive or even desperate and may alienate existing friends of your new acquaintance. At the same time, rushing friendships can cause messy situations if you move too fast and then find out you don't really like a person all that much.

Relating to Faculty

You have always been taught that we live in a democratic society, right? That may be so, but a college classroom is not really a democracy. A more accurate description might be a benevolent dictatorship—and that's if you are lucky enough to have a professor who believes in benevolence!

Perhaps a better analogy is to compare the classroom environment to a court of law. After all, the instructor sits in judgment of everything you do, say, or write, at least within the context of the course you are taking. As a result, your relationship tends to be a little skewed compared with dealings with friends and other peers. Knowing that the professor is constantly sizing you up in comparison to other students will probably engender some extra stress on top of the pressure of the work itself.

The better you understand what professors want to see in their students, the more effectively you can handle the stress of relating to faculty members. Although they may seem intimidating at first with their impressive academic credentials, it's a mistake to assume that all professors operate on some remote intellectual plane far above the lives of mere students. To the contrary, most professors are just like anyone else in that they have a job to do, and those who make that job easier will be well received. If you can assist in that process by avoiding the rough edges that instructors find as irritants in some students, you are almost sure to get ahead.

In the first place, don't assume that everyone who teaches a college class is a full professor with a Ph.D. or other terminal degree. College faculty vary enormously in background and credentials. Many faculty members hold master's degrees but have not earned doctorates, and you will err if you call every instructor "Dr." In addition, many institutions have ranking systems where faculty start out as instructors, move up to assistant professors, then associate professors, and finally full professors. A given faculty member may hold any of these ranks or may be working without rank as an adjunct (part-time) instructor or a graduate teaching assistant. The last named are still students and may have little or no previous teaching experience. The typical graduate assistant is someone working on a graduate degree who has been assigned to teach a freshman class or two.

All this diversity means more than just the need to be careful about how you address a faculty member (if they do not make it clear at the beginning of the term whether they want to be called "Dr.," "Mr.," "Ms.," or whatever, just ask). It also means you can't assume anything about previous teaching experience, ability to communicate information, attitude toward students, or any other characteristic about any single faculty member. Instead, the smart approach is to study each one the way you would a chapter in a book and then use the information whenever you need to interact with the instructor.

For instance, many instructors welcome students' questions in class. If something is not clear to you, it's in the best interest of you and everyone else in the class to speak up promptly and ask for clarification. Not only will you gain a better understanding of the issue at hand, but if handled properly this kind of interaction will make a favorable impression as you demonstrate your interest in the subject.

On the other hand, some faculty are annoyed by such questions, seeing them as interruptions to a carefully prepared lecture or evidence that you haven't read an assignment or thought about it carefully enough. And even those who encourage questions may become annoyed if you speak out too frequently or pose questions that sound trivial.

To avoid problems in this area, observe faculty members when other students ask questions or make comments in class. It doesn't take genius to read the facial expressions, voice tones, and comments of instructors, and then determine how they feel about the process. After ascertaining the preferred style, adjust your own behavior accordingly. This does not mean acting falsely or playing a role in each class, but simply observing the reality of basic differences in different people.

Some faculty don't mind being approached after class to explain a point, or having you drop by their offices. All have weekly office hours for conferences with students. As long as you observe basic courtesies and don't appear hostile or insolent, it's hard to go wrong in this process. Don't be shy about bringing up questions or concerns, for that is part of the role of the active student, and professors are used to dealing with students on all kinds of issues.

Most instructors do have pet peeves, however, and you can limit problems by avoiding them. You'll probably hear about some of them during the first session of the course or see them listed in the course syllabus. Whether it's making certain you never write in pencil, folding papers a certain way, or some other similar point, you can limit stress for you and your instructor by following instructions about such matters.

There are some basics that almost all faculty members notice. One of these is tardiness. Nobody likes to have a class interrupted by a student who comes in late, especially if that is a frequent violation by the same student. Coming late to class probably won't cause you to flunk, but it may damage the instructor's opinion of you, and that could make a substantial difference as the instructor deliberates over which grade to assign you on a paper or at the end of the course.

Professors also tend to be irritated by excuses or rationalizations. For example, students who miss class or forget an assignment and then insist on giving a detailed explanation often hurt their cases rather than helping them. Most professors don't care about your excuses or any other details about your personal life.

College faculty also expect you to have some consideration for their own work loads. If you turn in a long paper or beg to make up a missed exam just before grades are due, that will inconvenience the instructor and certainly won't win you any points for cooperation. Similarly, professors have their own problems and deadlines, and they don't want to listen to you complain about all the homework you have in other classes or gripe about the difficulties you might be facing in their class.

It's better to be anonymous than become labeled as an irritant. Try to look at the classroom situation from the faculty member's viewpoint, and you can avoid adding to your own stress problems unnecessarily.

Taking Advantage of Campus Resources

While the student's routine is filled with challenges, one advantage of college life is that plenty of help is available for those who need it. Colleges employ a variety of professionals specifically to provide support services to students. Almost every institution, from the smallest college to the largest university, offers some kind of organized program of student support (see the chart on the next page).

In fact, colleges can't become accredited—or keep their accreditation—unless they provide substantial opportunities for students to supplement the academic experience. As a result of these kinds of standards and as a matter of basic educational philosophy, the tuition you pay entitles you to much more than classroom instruction. This includes a variety of special services designed to help you cope with problems and succeed in college.

WHEN YOU NEED HELP . . .

Type of Assistance	Person or Office to Contact
General information; whom to see about a problem	Dean of Students, Vice President for Student Affairs or equivalent
Academic difficulties	Professors causing you trouble; special services such as math or writing labs; tutors; other students
Career advice	Career counseling center, if available; counselors
Course selection	Your academic adviser
Depression	School doctor or nurse; counselor
Homesickness	Counselors; fellow students
Illness	Campus health services
Job searches	Placement office
Math problems	Math professors; tutors; other students; math center if available
Money problems	Counselor (for general advice); Director of Financial Aid (for loan or scholarship help)
Personal problems	Counselors
Religious questions	Campus chaplain; representatives of various denominations who visit campus regularly
Roommate problems	Resident assistants or advisers; Director of Housing
Sources of academic information	Librarians
Transcripts	Registrar's office or student records office
Transfer information	Academic advisers; admission office staff at the school where you plan to transfer
Unfair treatment by a professor	Department head in the professor's academic department; dean or chief academic officer; academic appeals committee
Writing problems	English professors; tutors; other students; writing lab if available

Counselors

A key role of college counselors is to listen to your problems and help you cope with them. "In today's colleges, counselors are well equipped to respond to situations from the run of the mill to special problems," says Pamela Steinberger, dean of students at DeVry Institute of Technology in Atlanta, Georgia. "They're attuned to the needs of students, and they have been trained to be empathetic about the particular problems college students encounter."

This can include help with personal adjustment problems, anxiety, program selection and career guidance, among other things. Some institutions even offer group counseling on certain topics. At Iowa State University in Ames, Iowa, students can participate in free group counseling on such subjects as assertiveness, personal growth, reducing test anxiety, eating disorders, and career exploration.

Advisers

Academic advisers are individuals assigned to help you select the right courses, plan your overall class schedule for each term, and make other decisions regarding your academic progress. Usually, you will be assigned a single adviser who will work with you on a one-on-one basis throughout your collegiate career.

In most cases, these advisers are faculty members who include the job of advising students along with their other duties such as teaching, grading papers and exams, writing, conducting research, participating in committees, and keeping up in their field. So sometimes it can be difficult to catch them when they have time to spend with you. But having the benefit of such advice can be a wonderful asset, especially in the case of experienced professors who can help steer you away from mistakes such as signing up for the wrong math course, taking too many electives, or missing out on a deadline for adding or dropping a class.

A common mistake is bypassing advisers or placing too

little importance on their role. Students have been known to fake advisers' signatures on registration forms just to speed things up, or to contact their adviser only when a document needs to be signed. Instead of falling into this habit, make it a practice to consult with an adviser frequently throughout your college career.

If for any reason you don't feel comfortable with your adviser, or happen to get assigned to one who can never seem to be located, ask to be reassigned to another adviser. Make this request by contacting the department chairperson in your major area or the director of advising, if such a position exists at your school.

Some colleges have peer advising programs where you obtain advice from a fellow student instead of a professor or staff member. The students serving in this role have received special training in addition to having attended the institution long enough to know it well. An advantage of working with peer advisers is that the process tends to be less formal, and sometimes it is easier to relate to another student instead of a faculty member.

Tutors

If you have trouble in a specific course, you might need a different kind of help. Although some professors will be willing to put in extra time if you are having trouble with the subject they teach, others are less willing or simply don't have the time. A better alternative, in many cases, is to work with a tutor.

"Tutors can be great," Ohio State's Kyle Morgan says. "We have a special office for tutors on our campus, and any student can go there for help."

According to Morgan, starting early is a key to success with tutors. "If you start having trouble with a class, get a tutor early before you begin to flounder," she recommends. "If it turns out you don't need as much help as you thought, that's okay. You can stop whenever you want. But finding someone who can focus on your problems may be a lifesaver."

Not all colleges have offices for tutoring, but you can almost always find students willing to serve in this capacity. Just look for notes on bulletin boards or in the school paper, or post a note of your own advertising for a tutor. Or approach a bright student who seems to have a good grasp of the material you're studying, and hire her for a few hours of help.

Other Sources of Help

If you live in a dormitory, a person you can consult on a variety of matters is a *resident assistant*. This may be a student who has taken on the job as an extra duty, or it may be a staff member. In any case, resident assistants or other dormitory supervisors can help you deal with problems ranging from too much noise to an inability to get along with your roommate.

Campus medical staff are also available at most colleges and universities. Many larger schools offer round-the-clock medical help through health centers staffed by registered nurses and, in some cases, physicians. If you need help with stress-related problems (or other medical concerns, for that matter), you can obtain medications or other treatment.

Iowa State University, for example, has a Student Health Center that provides an array of services. Students may receive medical help in areas such as general medical care through an outpatient clinic, preventive medicine, gynecology, psychiatry, dermatology, diet counseling, and emergency services, among others.

Even smaller colleges usually offer some kind of medical or health services, although a full-fledged center may not be available. If you need help, a counselor or other staff member will refer you to qualified medical help available off-campus. Referral services are usually available for psychological matters as well as other medical assistance, often on a free or reduced-fee basis.

In addition to college or government-funded services, most schools sponsor or allow activities of a more religious nature in some form or another. Private, church-affiliated colleges often have a chaplain or other official who is available to help students through counseling, religious instruction, and other assistance.

Public colleges and universities do not offer such services directly, but many allow churches to send their own representatives on a voluntary basis. For example, at Longwood College in Farmville, Virginia, campus ministers represent Baptist, Episcopal, Catholic, Presbyterian, and Methodist churches. In addition, religiously oriented student organizations include the Baptist Student Union, Campus Christian Fellowship, Wesley Foundation, Catholic Student Association, Inter-Religious Council, and the Canterbury Association.

Calling on your religious faith can provide real comfort when you're feeling stressed. And if you're not a religious person, you will have the option of checking out various faiths or religious organizations if you would like.

Special Programs Services

In addition to the usual array of counseling and related services, many colleges offer special academic support programs to help students cope with the demands of college-level work.

For example, Smith College, a private institution in Northampton, Massachusetts, helps students learn to write and study more effectively through its Center for Academic Development. Students receive free one-on-one instruction from the center's writing counselors, who review papers in draft form, pinpoint strengths and weaknesses, and suggest improvements.

Miami-Dade Community College, a public two-year college in Miami, Florida, offers a wide range of services through its Challenge Center. Combining counseling, advising, and tutorial services, the center uses an integrated approach to help students surmount academic problems and other difficulties. Miami-Dade also offers an English Language Institute, which helps students whose native language is not English master the language skills necessary for success in college.

If you are a minority student, handicapped, or a student who may be considered disadvantaged because of economic reasons, you may be eligible for special programs designed to increase the chances for success in college. One of these is the U.S. Department of Education's Special Services for Disadvantaged Students program, which provides unique services at several hundred colleges and universities through grants to the institutions. If you qualify to participate in one of these campus-based programs, you can obtain a variety of services such as free tutoring, special counseling, and cultural enrichment programs.

The federal government also supports a variety of other services at colleges and universities that have applied for and received grants for such purposes. For example, some colleges offer special support services though the Health Careers Opportunities Program, which exists to help students succeed in pursuing careers in the health sciences. Similar programs are offered at various colleges in nursing and other fields.

Locating Resources

Orientation

Where do you find the right sources of assistance? One of the best places to start is any orientation program for new students. If your college offers an orientation program, don't skip it. Even if you have to make a special trip to campus, the time will be well spent as you learn basic facts about the programs and services available.

Some orientation programs last a full day or more, involving parents as well as incoming students. Other more streamlined versions take only a couple of hours. In either case, the information provided can prove invaluable.

At Bluefield State College in Bluefield, West Virginia, each new student participates in an individualized, one-on-one advising session during the summer before the first semester of collegiate studies. This meeting with a faculty member or college administrator usually lasts about 90 minutes, and the student gets the chance to pose any questions as well as to set up his or her schedule of classes.

Other colleges, such as the University of Missouri, sponsor programs where experienced students work with new students to help get them oriented to campus. Still others hold group sessions where various speakers present information you will need in learning your way around campus.

Catalogs

Another source of information is the college catalog. A catalog is more than just a publication to review when you're selecting a school. Instead, it's the single best source of facts about academic policies, requirements, and rights you have as a student. Sure, no college catalog makes exciting reading, but be sure to obtain a catalog, read it carefully, and keep it for future reference. In acquainting yourself with the rules, regulations, and deadlines that dominate academic life at any institution, you can avoid some stressful problems.

When I was an undergraduate, I made the mistake of failing to read carefully the section of the catalog dealing with requirements for majors and minors. I was seeking a bachelor's degree with a major in English and a minor in history. I had noted that the catalog said at least 30 semester hours in a discipline were required for a major, and 15 hours for a minor. By my senior year I had piled up over 40 hours in English classes and 15 hours in history, and thought I was right on target to graduation. But then an administrator pointed out that I needed *two* minors to graduate, not just one. When I said that I'd never heard of that rule, he simply referred me to the catalog and sure enough there it was, in black and white.

67

Fortunately, I was able to pick up enough appropriate courses in my senior year to complete a second minor in political science, and graduated that year according to my original goal. But without some luck and a cooperative assistant dean who allowed me to switch some courses several weeks into the semester, my graduation would have been delayed for a semester or maybe even an entire academic year—all because I failed to read the catalog carefully!

When looking over a catalog, don't be put off by the volume of material included. Most of it applies to specific curriculums, including a description of every course offered by each department. Just be sure to read the sections on the programs in which you are interested, as well as the general information about academic regulations, special programs and services, and similar details. Many catalogs also include a listing of faculty along with their degrees and where they earned them, which can help you learn more about your instructors.

Handbooks

Student handbooks provide details similar to those in college catalogs, the main difference being an emphasis on student policies and services rather than program descriptions. In recent years, more and more colleges have begun to incorporate handbooks as a part of their catalogs, but others still publish them as separate documents. They're usually distributed at registration for fall classes.

You can find all kind of potential information in handbooks, so be sure to read yours. Some of the content may be a bit on the legalistic side, such as what procedures are used for disciplining students and what your rights are if you feel you've received unfair academic treatment. Other details may include a description of social groups such as fraternities, sororities, honor societies, and special interest clubs, along with information on student government. Still other details might cover counseling services, career guidance and placement opportunities, and a list of intramural sports.

Other Sources of Help

Many other special programs and services are advertised through announcements on bulletin boards, notices in student newspapers, handouts in class, and other means.

If you're not sure where to turn for help, check with the student affairs office. This office will have different names on different campuses: Student Services, Student Affairs, Dean of Students' Office, Vice President for Student Affairs, or something similar. Whatever it's called, this is the place where student support services are administered. The personnel working in this office will know which services are available, where to go to locate them, and the names of the right people with whom to talk.

Special Courses and Workshops

Along with the subjects covered on a one-to-one basis, you can take advantage of special workshops and short courses designed to help you with various problems. Most of these are offered on a noncredit basis so there is no need to worry about grades or performance, and many are free to students.

For instance, Gannon University in Erie, Pennsylvania, offers a special program through its Office of New Student Services on "Reaching Your Academic and Personal Potential." This program includes sessions on getting off to a good start in college; mastering the essentials of reading textbooks; effective note taking; and learning how to "ace" exams. Sessions are offered once a week during the first month of class, and each one is taught by a different member of the university's student affairs staff.

Similar programs may be found at other colleges and universities. Attending a few such sessions will be well worth the minimal amount of time invested.

Stress and the Big Three: Drugs, Sex, and Alcohol

If you want to conduct an experiment in stress, just mention to a parent the great drugs, alcohol, or sex available at the college you have selected. Watch for changes in facial expression or tone of voice, and you will almost certainly get a mini-lesson in how a parent deals with stress!

From the student's point of view, however, these three subjects constitute a major area of potential stress. The relative freedom of college life also can bring challenges in dealing with these highly personal and potentially explosive issues.

The simplest advice about drugs and alcohol would be just to stay away from either commodity. And a similar argument can be made about sex. But that ignores the realities of contemporary college life. Unless you live a sheltered life, chances are you will find yourself encountering situations involving drugs, alcohol, and sexual relations. What do you do if someone pressures you to join in the "fun" at a party when this means trying some "recreational" drugs? What if you discover your roommate has a drinking problem? How do you handle the pressures exerted by someone who wants to be not just a friend but a lover? Or what if your standards of sexual conduct are stricter than those of some of your friends, and they keep giving you a hard time about it?

Most college students must tackle questions such as these sooner or later. How they are answered will depend on your own religious or moral beliefs, family upbringing, and previous experiences. Ultimately they come down to individual choice. But from a stress management angle, the following advice is offered for your consideration:

1. *Never use chemicals as a way of dealing with stress.* Too often, alcohol and drugs are touted as a way of relaxing. A few drinks or a pill (or other drug delivery system) are seen as an avenue for making you feel less tense and helping worries

disappear. But they really contribute to stress rather than alleviate it. After all, drugs can cause all kinds of physical and emotional problems which sooner or later will heighten stress. The price for that temporary feeling of euphoria can range from a splitting headache to permanent damage to the kidneys, heart, brain, or other vital organs. And alcohol or drug use too often leads to addiction, not just in older people after years of use, but in college students who never imagined a little "recreation" would lead to becoming an alcoholic or an addict. Whether the result is physical damage or addiction (or both), the pain and anxiety that follow will only increase your stress burden.

In addition to the direct physical and emotional damage anyone can suffer from chemical abuse, students face special dangers. When you're under the influence of drugs, judgment is impaired, and a student with poor judgment is like a soldier whose rifle sights are badly bent. Even though you'd like to hit the target, it's virtually impossible. If you're trying to take an exam or absorb important lecture information while drugs are in your system, your mind simply won't operate efficiently, and you may perform very badly without even realizing it. In addition, there is always the risk of being noticed by a professor, administrator, or campus security officer, with disciplinary action a possibility. Even if you stay totally away from drugs during class time but think it's okay to partake during evenings or weekends, stop and reassess. Chances are you will neglect your studies as a result and suffer academic as well as physical problems.

When it comes to drinking or taking drugs, the following steps can make good sense for anyone:

—If you have not yet experimented, don't start. You're really not missing anything but potential trouble.

—If you play around but still feel in complete control, don't push your luck. Just because problems have not yet developed, don't assume you are invulnerable. You're not.

—If chemical dependency has already become a worry, do something about it now instead of letting the problem grow worse. The medical services provided by your college (either directly or through referral services to local physicians, chemical abuse specialists, or clinics) can help you turn things around, if you don't feel you can change your behavior without some assistance.

—Increase your knowledge base. Do you really understand the physiological effects of drugs? Much of what you "know" may in fact be incorrect information picked up from friends, television, or popular literature. The conventional wisdom may be that marijuana is harmless, for example. But recent research has demonstrated several types of genuine damage marijuana causes to the body. For this or other drugs, make sure your knowledge is adequate by reading up-to-date books, magazine articles, or other materials that provide accurate information. Or talk to a doctor, nurse, therapist, or other informed person. But don't sell yourself short through a simple lack of knowledge.

—Never forget that your main goal is to succeed. College will be hard enough without the physical and psychological problems caused by substances your body was not designed to use.

2. *If you are pressured to experiment with drugs or alcohol, say no.* Even elementary school students have been taught the very good advice of "just say no." The strategy is equally valid for college students. Holding out against this kind of social pressure will probably be stressful, but it's stress you can handle. At least you will stay in control of your own life, which is more than can be guaranteed if you give in.

To limit stress caused by saying no, try measures such as these:

—Don't call undue attention to your decision not to use drugs or alcohol. It's one thing to quietly decline, but quite another to make a big deal of it. Instead of launching into a major lecture about the evils of chemicals, just say "no thanks" or "I'd rather not." Or volunteer to be the one to drive if the situation warrants it. Stick to your decision, but don't open yourself up to a debate or a position where you seem to be staking a claim for some kind of moral superiority.

One of the oldest tricks used by nondrinkers in social situations is to nurse a drink just like everyone else, but to make sure it is nonalcoholic such as soda water or a soft drink. That way, you don't look out of place if others around you are drinking, but you remain in total control of yourself.

—Avoid high-pressure situations. If you really want to play it smart, try to avoid social events where drug use or heavy drinking is the norm. This is not always possible, but sometimes the easiest way to say no is simply avoiding the opportunity in the first place. For instance, if it is obvious that a party is turning into a drug fest, leave early. Or if your roomie not only drinks all the time but always nags you to join in, maybe it's time to find a new roommate.

—Take strength in numbers. Believe it or not, when you say no you will not be the only one taking such a stance. Other students will be heading in the same direction. To ease the difficulty of peer pressure, find students who feel the same as you and spend some time with them. As friendships develop, you'll find that you can enjoy a social life that is just as full as anyone else's, but minus the presence of unwanted chemicals.

3. *Don't treat sex casually.* Whatever you do, always treat sex as serious business. Don't fall victim to the false illusion that you are now totally free and can do whatever you wish. Sexual relations can result in highly stressful emotional entanglements, not to mention serious physical diseases. Whatever your own particular beliefs about the morality side of this issue, be sure to keep in mind the very real problems that can develop. Just for a start, such problems can include:

—Sexually transmitted diseases, ranging from simple infections to fatal illnesses such as AIDS.

—Emotional stress resulting from broken relationships, jealousy, and other conflicts that can arise in an intense relationship.

—Inner conflict resulting from clashes in value systems (for example, you have always been taught that premarital sex is wrong, but you go ahead and become involved in sexual relationships—and then find yourself struggling with a heavy sense of guilt).

—Unplanned pregnancies and the whole range of potential related crises (abortions, sudden marriages, financial problems, decisions to leave college, and other possibilities).

Of course, these are some of the *bad* things that can result from sexual relationships. Obviously there is a positive side to this basic element of human existence! But since the negatives are what cause stress problems, the point is to limit such problems through wise choices and smart actions. The decisions will be yours to make, and no one else's. From a stress management viewpoint, never overlook the importance of following your head and not just your emotions.

4. *Get help if you need it.* If drug or alcohol use is already a problem in your life, or problems of a sexual nature are bothering you, get help in dealing with your problem. As mentioned earlier in this chapter, every campus has counselors and other trained professionals who will provide the assistance you need. If they can't help you, they will refer you to someone who can. Your privacy will be protected in the process, and you can face your own situation with the help of people who know and understand the problems college students face in this area.

CHAPTER 6

*M*ANAGING
TIME BETTER

*I*f you've ever stayed up late at night meeting the deadline for a paper or cramming for an exam, you have experienced the stress caused by poor time management. "If only I had started earlier," you might have sighed to yourself as the clock ticked inexorably on, and the pressure mounted.

Of course, your time is limited. But the truth is that you have just as much time as any other person, and it's how you manage your time that really counts.

"If you want to be a successful student, you need to develop good time management skills," advises Dr. Sue Bruning, an assistant professor of administrative sciences at Kent State University in Ohio. "It's very important to get in the habit of setting priorities and deciding how much time to devote to each task you must accomplish. Some things will naturally take more time than others, and it's up to you to manage your time wisely."

Taking Stock of Commitments

As a first step in improving your time management skills, take a close look at how you are spending your time now. Let's say you sleep roughly eight hours a night. (Don't worry if your routine includes more or less sleep than this "average" amount; very few people actually grab an eight-hour block of snooze time daily.) That leaves 16 hours a day to cover everything else in your life. Exactly how are you spending those hours?

For Paul, a sophomore at a large public university, every hour is committed. He is taking a 19-hour class load that includes, physics, calculus, and German, all required courses in his engineering curriculum. The classroom time and homework alone would be enough to keep busy, but that is only the start of Paul's schedule. He also works 15 hours a week at the help station in the university computer center, plays trumpet in the jazz band, writes for the university paper, and participates in the computing club and the engineering society.

Does this mean Paul is headed for trouble? It could be, but he has avoided serious stress problems by making smart use of his time. Instead of just letting commitments pile up until he has exceeded his capacity for handling them, Paul has carefully assessed the amount of time available to him and decided how many hours he can devote to each activity. He also has considered past experience and his own particular abilities for getting things done. As a result, he has found he can maintain a very heavy schedule without becoming overworked.

Paul has also taken advantage of several effective strategies for managing time. In the first place, he developed a time management log and identified pockets of wasted time, and then eliminated much of the waste. He has made careful plans for accomplishing important tasks such as research papers and other academic assignments. And he has utilized efficient approaches for taking notes, organizing study material, and saving time through word processing, among other time management techniques described later in this chapter. The end result is that he can accomplish a great deal and still have adequate time for fun and relaxation. Of course, not every student can manage such a heavy workload, but everyone can improve efficiency through the use of careful management of time.

Avoiding Academic Overload

A sure path to stress is taking too many classes in any given term. The question is, how many courses are too many?

If there were a single answer to this question, all college students would face the same limit on just how heavy an academic load they could carry. But policies vary from one college to another, and within these guidelines the choice is normally up to the individual student.

For colleges operating on the semester system, an hour of credit is roughly equivalent to an hour spent in the classroom every week for 14 to 16 weeks. A lecture-based course worth three credits might meet three times a week for an hour each time, or twice weekly for an hour and a half, or in the case of night classes, once a week for three hours (actually, the time for each hour is usually around 50 minutes, but for discussion purposes the difference is insignificant).

It gets a little more complicated for laboratory classes, which are considered a kind of practice and thus not of equivalent weight to lecture time. You might have to put in two or three "clock" hours a week to one hour of credit in laboratory courses.

The most common college courses are worth three semester hours of credit. Typical classes in English, history, the social sciences, and many others follow this pattern. Some science courses are worth four credits, often combining a laboratory component with lecture sessions. Still others may be worth only one or two credits (examples include physical education activity courses, career planning courses, and others). A few others, such as some nursing courses, internships, and other special courses, may carry five semester hours of credit or more.

Given this framework, the combination of courses selected by students will vary widely. One student might take six courses for a total of 14 credit hours, while another might take only five courses but earn a total of 18 hours' credit.

At most colleges, you must take at least 12 semester hours to be considered a full-time student. This is the minimum load you should consider for any semester unless you plan on taking five or six years to earn a bachelor's degree, since you will need to average about 15 or 16 hours a semester to graduate in eight semesters; or unless you make up the difference by attending summer sessions. Even at that, enrolling for only 12 hours is dangerous, because if for any reason you have to withdraw from a course your status would change to that of a part-time student, and you could lose financial aid, athletic eligibility, or other benefits where full-time student status is required.

At the upper end of the scale, you probably will not be allowed to take more than 18 credits without special permission. For a freshman, this will normally be difficult to obtain, although experienced college students occasionally enroll for 20 hours or more. This is the exception rather than the rule, however, and most educators argue against it.

Ideally, your own load should fall somewhere between the two. Fifteen to 17 hours may be the best load, one which shouldn't cause an unmanageable amount of work but will keep you on track toward graduation within a reasonable time. Of course, it all depends on the content of the courses you are taking, along with other factors such as whether you are working part-time.

At any rate, keep in mind that each extra hour of credit

means more time in course preparation. According to an old standard, you should plan on putting in at least two hours of studies for every credit hour for which you are enrolled. So a 15-hour load can translate to a 45-hour work week. That's enough to keep anyone busy!

To succeed in college, you will probably want to avoid a schedule like Paul's. Instead, you will want to maintain a load you know you can handle. Too much activity—whether mental, physical, or a combination–will wear you down sooner or later. Instead, manage your time effectively to head off stress problems. If you fail to use this precious commodity wisely, it's easy to become frustrated as work piles up and you begin to wonder how you will get it all done.

Develop a Time Management Diary

One way to get an idea of how well you're managing time is to keep a log of your activities every day for a week or so during your first term in college. (Or if you're still in high school but plan on attending college, go ahead and try this now as a dry run). Write down every task and then beside each entry, record the time involved. Do this for every activity or effort—not just major items such as writing a term paper or attending class, but time spent talking with a friend, washing your hair, watching a television show, and so forth. Include every way you spend your time, even if it seems trivial. Lunch, breaks between classes, time spent reading the newspaper or a paperback novel—everything counts (see sample).

After a few days, review your record carefully. You might be surprised at how little time was actually spent on class work and how much was spent on other activities. In fact, if you're like most students, you probably will find several hours a day that seem to have escaped you, like fleeting recollections of answers to the world's hardest test.

Once you get a feel for how much time is wasted, you can

SAMPLE ACTIVITY LOG

Activity/October 4	Starting Time	Ending Time	Comments
Showering/Dressing	7:05	7:45	
Breakfast	7:45	7:50	Doughnuts on the run
Walked to class	7:50	7:57	
English 101	8:00	8:50	
Sociology	9:00	9:50	
Talked with friends in Student Center	10:00	10:50	
Computer class	11:00	11:50	
Lunch with Susan	12:00	1:00	Sat on steps and relaxed
Watched TV soaps	1:00	2:00	
Walked to chemistry lab	2:00	2:05	Lab canceled
Went back to dorm/ listened to music	2:15	4:00	
Fell asleep	4:00	5:00	
Went for walk	5:00	5:15	
Dinner in cafeteria	5:20	6:10	
Went to library	6:15	7:45	Worked on research paper
Phoned Anne	7:45	8:00	
Watched TV	8:10	11:00	
Wrote letter home	11:00	11:25	
Watched "Tonight Show"	11:30	12:30	
Went to bed	12:30		

ACTIVITY LOG

Activity/Day	Time	Time	Comments

use the results of this study as a guide for restructuring your daily routine. Even the smallest efforts to make your day more productive will pay off if followed regularly.

Set Priorities

Sure, you want to make good grades. Or at the very least, you want to pass all your classes. But in attempting to make the most of your opportunities as a student, it's easy to lose perspective on which tasks are most important. By setting priorities and then concentrating efforts on those at the top of the list, though, you can virtually guarantee results.

According to Kent State's Dr. Bruning, it's important not just to establish priorities but to write them down. "Writing things down helps crystallize your thinking and re-enforce goals that matter the most," she notes. "Once you commit a list of priority items to writing, you can then devote your attention to them accordingly. You can also go back to them and re-evaluate the priorities as needed."

For example, write down the 10 most important assignments or tasks you must complete this week. Then spend the bulk of your time completing the top two or three, rather than committing an equal amount of time on each of the 10 assignments. In reality those items at the bottom of the list can probably wait until later, and the truly important work will be accomplished more rapidly.

Learn to Say No

It's important for you to try to avoid that deathtrap of the conscientious student: overcommitment. All you must do is learn to say no.

Of course, this is easier said than done. But to protect yourself from being stressed out by too many commitments, learn to say no to some of the demands for your time.

This might mean simply avoiding being the one who volunteers when a professor asks for someone to do an oral report on the South African political system. Or it might mean turning down a chance to act in a college revival of *West Side Story* that happens to coincide with the semester you have to take advanced French and calculus. Protect your own best interests by refusing to allow yourself to become overstressed by taking on every request or opportunity that comes your way.

Make Careful Plans

In a student's sometimes hectic world, poor planning often leads to crisis situations. And crisis almost always leads to stress.

You can avoid both by making careful planning a basic part of your academic routine. There are all kinds of ways to conduct planning, but most will depend on your developing some kind of written system to keep tabs on everything you must accomplish.

Some students depend heavily on lists of assignments due tomorrow, projects to accomplish this week, or similar information. There are almost as many formats for this as there are students. If you haven't already developed such a system, try one or more of the following:

1. *Keep a spiral notebook for each class.* Take care to write down in the notebook every homework assignment, upcoming exam, reading assignment, and other important tasks. Then use a bright marker (yellow is best) to highlight any notes about assignments and deadlines. Make it a practice to read over each highlighted section every night so you don't over-

look anything or let a long-range deadline slip up on you. When an assignment has been completed, place a check mark beside it.

2. *Make use of an inexpensive appointment calendar.* This is the kind that business people rely on to keep track of their appointments. Make certain that it's not a small pocket-sized version, but rather one large enough to provide a good amount of space for each day of the year. Then for each day, write notes about anything that's due. Instead of dividing things by subject area, include everything together on a daily basis. This helps you keep an idea of "the big picture" rather than concentrating too much on one subject to the exclusion of others.

For this to work to best effect, make multiple entries for long-term projects such as term papers or completion of extensive reading assignments. If a paper is due in six weeks, note dates when your preliminary research should be done, when the first draft should be completed, when the final typing should be started, and so forth. If you have to read *Tom Jones*, set dates for finishing the book in increments of 100 or 200 pages. A simple system of writing down and following target dates can provide an effective planning framework.

3. *Develop or adapt a calendar program for your computer.* This tool provides the same function as an appointment calendar but handles the task electronically. The computer can do a great job of reminding you about deadlines and flagging your attention to follow up on tasks you have noted as important.

4. *Use self-sticking notes as reminders.* For an impending assignment, upcoming quiz, or other task, place self-sticking notes in a prominent spot such as on your mirror or on the wall above your desk. These may be the best invention since pizza! Most are bright colored so it is hard to miss them, and they come in various sizes. And they're inexpensive too.

If none of this fits your personality, develop your own system. With careful organization, you can assume more control of your academic life and avoid bouts with crisis situations.

Don't Cut Classes

One area where you should make optimum use of your time is class attendance. Most students simply assume they'll attend class regularly, just as they always have. But then they encounter the freedom of the collegiate environment and a new temptation: cutting classes.

If you want to make the best use of your time, go to class regularly. Don't fall into the trap of skipping classes, even though in college this is a convenient way to make life easier on any given day.

Why do so many college students fall into the habit of skipping classes? The main reason is that nobody really seems to care. You can get way with it to a degree never dreamed of in high school, where teachers keep detailed attendance records and unexplained absences are cause for discipline. At the college level, you are expected to take responsibility for whether or not you attend classes. Instead of heading for the classroom, you can be sleeping late, soaking up some late morning sun, or catching the latest installment of your favorite soap, without any immediate consequences. There seldom is someone keeping an eye on your activities the way a parent or high school teacher might.

Even those professors who make a point about attendance—and many don't even check—probably won't hassle you about it. In some situations, you can get by without problems as long as you perform well on tests and assignments. But other professors will exact penalties, ranging from refusal to let you make up work you have missed, to dismissal from the class because of excessive absences. If you happen to have cut class the day a professor announces those rules, by the time you realize you're in trouble, it may be too late.

The safe approach, of course, is simply not to cut classes, even those you find frustrating or boring. Try to discipline yourself to attend every session so you will not miss lectures, in-class assignments, quizzes, or other important work. The next best option, if you feel compelled to exercise your freedom, is to play it smart in selecting classes to miss. For example, allow yourself no more than one or two cuts in each course so the negative impact is spread out, rather than missing several class sessions in one course. Make it a point not to take cuts early in the term, or you could run into difficulty later if you must miss due to illness. And when you are out of class, arrange to get notes and class instructions from a friend *before* the next class meeting. There are few worse situations in college than returning from an absence and finding that an exam or oral report has been scheduled for the day!

Establish Regular Study Times

In addition to planning ahead for long-term projects, be sure to set up regular times for completing your academic assignments. By making studying a regular part of your daily routine, you can avoid the tendency to put off work and the problems that invariably result.

One factor working in your favor is the way college classes are scheduled. Unlike high school where your classes follow one another in a tightly scheduled day, college classes usually span a wider time frame, with most students having several free periods between their classes. For instance, you might begin the day with a class at 8 a.m., followed immediately by another from 9 to 10. But your next class might not meet until 1 p.m. What do you do with the time between? Part will be needed for lunch, but the rest will be at your own discretion. Students find all kinds of ways to fill up such times, including playing video games, watching television, or just hanging out in the student center. But a smarter approach is to use this time for class preparation. It's not a matter of "all work and no play," either. The time you spend here will keep you from being overloaded later, and by working at assignments gradually for an hour here and an hour there, you can avoid the stress of having too much work due at the same time.

Try a Few Night Classes

Most full-time students take their classes during the day, whereas part-time students, especially working adults, attend primarily during the evening. But if you'd like to spread out your schedule and give yourself more free time during the day, why not enroll in an occasional night class? This isn't for everybody, but for some students evening classes help prevent the feeling of being overloaded. This is especially true if you work a part-time job during the day and feel there just aren't enough hours of daylight to get everything done.

The hours spent in class end up being the same, but the advantage of this trade-off is simply spreading out the class time in a way that may be more convenient for your personal schedule. If you don't have a heavy load of daytime commitments, this option might not be attractive to you.

A fringe benefit of night classes is that the amount of work assigned is sometimes slightly less than in day classes. Night classes ostensibly cover exactly the same material as those scheduled any other time, but in reality this is not always the case. Some professors give fewer term papers or other out-of-class assignments in their evening classes. If you're juggling the work of several tough classes, this can provide a little breathing room.

Increase Your Reading Efficiency

Much of the work required in college consists of reading. English instructors will pile on essays, short stories, plays, and novels. History professors may assign hundreds of pages of historical readings. Faculty members in every discipline from physics to economics will make reading assignments a basic component of your academic work.

Virtually every class requires a textbook, and many require several additional books. Add to this the reading necessary to complete research assignments, term papers, and other work, and it's difficult to overemphasize the importance of efficient reading skills to your overall success as a student.

If you can improve your reading efficiency, you can save time, accomplish more work, and reduce the stress of fulfilling assignments. Try to develop two different reading styles: a speedy version where you cover a lot of material in a short time and a more concentrated version where you soak up every word. Use the former for background reading and less important material, and save the latter for textbook reading, especially that which you expect to form the basis of exams.

You can also build skills in this area by taking special courses available on many campuses. You may be able to improve reading skills substantially by taking a single course or seminar on this subject.

Grab "Stolen Moments"

As your time management diary will probably show, a certain amount of your time is lost in the gaps between major activities. But much of this nonproductive time could be used profitably. If you develop a habit of grabbing "stolen moments" from your daily routine, you can get more work accomplished while still leaving adequate time for fun and relaxation.

For example, a doctor's appointment almost guarantees a long stint in the waiting room. Instead of killing time reading magazines or watching other patients, take advantage of these extra minutes—or hours—by reading that novel required in your English literature class. Or tackle one of your textbook reading assignments, complete some math problems, or work on the outline for a paper or report. Even small amounts of work accomplished will add up and cut down on the hours you must put in later.

The same strategy applies for time spent at the hairdresser or barber, dentist, laundromat, auto shop, or anywhere else you find yourself sitting and waiting.

If you experiment with a time management diary for at least a week, try adding up all the minutes and hours of the "gaps" in your schedule. (You might want to develop a work sheet like the one that follows). An extra hour or two a day, compounded over several weeks, would provide enough extra time to complete a superb research paper, read several books, or otherwise make a huge dent in your work load.

Save Time with Computers

One of the most effective time-savers is the computer. It's such a big help, in fact, that some colleges and universities require every incoming freshman to buy a personal computer along with the books and other supplies needed to begin college.

Even if your school does not have such a requirement, you will probably end up taking at least one class about computers. Computer literacy has become as basic as reading, writing, and arithmetic, and your chances of earning a degree without picking up some computer skills are pretty limited.

Too many students, though, treat their knowledge of computers as something to be applied later in their professional lives rather than as a tool to make college life easier. Yet there is no better tool for helping you make maximum use of your time.

At the very least, make certain that you master word processing. You can save a huge amount of time by using

WORKSHEET FOR STEALING TIME

Step 1: Complete daily activity log (time management diary) for at least one week.

Step 2: Add to obtain daily totals of time spent in unproductive ways.

Step 3: Add daily totals of "wasted" time to obtain weekly estimate of time available for better usage.

Step 4: Dedicate *part* of unused time to studies or useful activity. (Note: always leave *some* unstructured time for fun and relaxation.)

	Day	Activity	Time Spent
1.			
2.			
3.			
4.			
5.			
6.			
7.			
			TOTAL:

word processing instead of a typewriter. This is true whether you are already a skilled typist or can barely bang out a few words. Working with a keyboard and monitor allows you to make unlimited mistakes and then correct them before a single word appears on paper. Such flexibility can help you avoid the stress of struggling with a manuscript and then having to retype material because you left out a sentence or simply made too many errors. Instead of screaming into a pillow and then starting over, you simply make the changes electronically—and painlessly!

Even if your typing skills are first-rate, word processing will increase your efficiency by allowing you to type faster, since a keyboard does not hold you back the way a typewriter does (there is no "catch-up" factor as you wait for a mechanical mechanism to strike paper, and one line will wrap into the next automatically without the delay of moving from one line to the next). The more efficient you become, the less time it takes to complete work, and the stress that results from feeling overloaded can be reduced or eliminated.

In addition, you can produce a completely new document by editing an old one, as opposed to starting from scratch. For instance, say you wrote a 12-page paper last semester on Franklin Roosevelt for your American history class, and now your political science professor has assigned you to write a five-page paper on any aspect of the U.S. Supreme Court. Since your previous paper included a section on Roosevelt's impact on the Supreme Court, you simply make an electronic copy of that section, edit and expand it using your word processing program, and you have a finished paper in perhaps half the time it would have otherwise taken. When you get used to this strategy, it can be a real stress fighter, especially after you have built up a bank of documents that can be used to help get a jump on new assignments.

Word processing also allows you to develop an outline and then fill it in item by item; to move sentences, paragraphs, or larger blocks of information freely within a document or from one document to another; and to revise material over and over without the agony of retyping the finished product. And a real lifesaver is the spell-checking option provided by most word processing programs. The computer will check every word of your paper or report and flag those spelled incorrectly. You just fix the mistakes, print out your copy, and it looks good—even if you're the Western Hemisphere's worst speller!

Computers also prove invaluable for projects required in science, engineering, and accounting classes, among others. Any task involving numbers or calculations will be made easier by a computer, not to mention design projects, organization of notes, bibliographies, and many other efforts.

Does this mean you must buy a personal computer to get along in college? Not necessarily, unless your campus is one of those few requiring you to purchase a machine when you enroll. You can probably tap into the institution's computer system by using terminals provided in the computer center or other locations, or you can make use of a computer lab where personal computers are provided for student use. Some colleges rent computers to students, whereas others provide them through their libraries or in other settings. Of course, owning your own computer is the most convenient, and today's systems are increasingly affordable. In any case, however you obtain access to a computer, be sure to use it to increase your capabilities for making smart use of time. The old cliché says time is money. For the serious college student, time means more than dollars—it means the capability for completing work and mastering material. By saving time through the use of computers, you can limit the prospects of overload and the stress that almost always accompanies it.

Develop Effective Note-Taking Techniques

One of the most demanding and important tasks is taking notes during class or while studying. For this to be productive and reassuring rather than stressful, you will need a well-organized system instead of just writing things down haphazardly.

An efficient way to take notes is using index cards instead of paper. The advantage of note cards is that you need not work sequentially. In other words, you are not bounded by the order in which material is committed to paper, and you can insert additional material easily.

Small index cards are convenient because they fit easily into a jacket pocket or the corner of a book bag, but they can be difficult to write on unless your handwriting is small and neat. You can't get very much information on a single 3-by-5-inch card, so larger 5-by-8-inch cards may be your best bet. They provide the main advantages of smaller cards plus more space, and are easier to write on when you're in a hurry or are trying to keep a single list on one card.

Be sure to keep the index cards for different courses or projects separate from each other to avoid the anxiety of having to sort through them, wondering if all the information you need is in one place. Using a different colored set of cards for each course is one way to ward off this problem. Another is simply to jot the initial of the course in the upper right corner as you use each card. You can also buy inexpensive folders designed especially for index cards.

At any rate, don't make the mistake of overdoing the amount of material you put into note form. Try to concentrate on the most important points covered in class or on written materials you are summarizing, rather than writing down every single detail. Otherwise, you can get bogged down from the sheer volume involved. You might find yourself scrambling to complete your notes in the first place and then inundated with more material than you can absorb when it comes time to study for an exam. For greatest efficiency, make sure any notes you take leave out unnecessary information. Use short phrases instead of whole sentences, and abbreviations or your own personal form of shorthand to keep notes concise and manageable.

Organize Your Information

Once you have information, whether that means notes or other material, you must be able to find it when needed. And that requires organization. Sounds simple, doesn't it? But how many times have you found yourself scrounging through piles of papers to find a single scrap of information? A basic part of avoiding the stress of such situations is good organization of notes, papers, course syllabuses, and other information.

Probably the simplest method is using a separate folder for each class you take, or a notebook containing vinyl pouches for your index cards. Keep everything related to the course in it, including class handouts and the course syllabus. Or you can put together a file system to be stored in a cabinet, file box, or plastic storage crate.

Whatever system you develop for maintaining printed materials, make sure it includes the following components:

- A logical and consistent pattern for arranging material. For example, within folders or notebooks, date all class notes and then arrange them in chronological order. Or create topic headings and put them in alphabetical order.

- Identification of each piece of paper. Just as you mark each note card so that it can be identified if separated from others, make sure any papers you keep (class handouts, photocopies of articles or portions of books, compositions written in draft form, and other materials) are marked with a brief identifier such as the name of the class for which they may be of use.

- A single place to keep study materials. Try to keep all papers, folders, and other class materials in one desk or another single location where you can retrieve them. Don't make the mistake of keeping some things in the closet, others on a desktop, others in a dresser drawer, and so on.

- Currency of information. As each semester or quarter passes and you enroll for new classes, set aside materials from previous terms. Avoid mingling current class papers with older ones from previous courses. Instead, use a box or extra shelf space to store older papers if you think they might prove useful later. Much can be thrown away, but if you feel better about keeping old work, at least keep it in the background.

A more elaborate system is possible with computers. One major advantage here is that computers have almost infinite capacity for storing this kind of information. It doesn't even matter how much memory your machine provides, as long as you can keep filling up diskettes. One diskette can store hundreds of pages of notes, and diskettes are cheap and readily available.

A problem with computers, though, is that you have to key in everything before it is usable. That can be a workable system, especially if you're already experienced with computers and have developed efficient keyboard skills. On the other hand, putting everything on a computer may be more trouble than it's worth, especially if you're working from handwritten notes, photocopies, or other printed information. In that case, using a computer may cause more stress than it avoids! It may be much more efficient to bypass the computer for certain tasks and spend your time reading and absorbing information instead of manipulating it.

Even if you do rely heavily on a computer, it will be important to develop some type of organizational system. Take time to label diskettes, name electronically stored documents in a way that they can be easily retrieved, and store information in such a manner that you won't waste time looking for it when needed. For example, you can give each document a name or a number and then list it in a notebook or on an index card, along with a brief description of the contents of the document. Another method is to use the computer itself to create a library or index of documents. Many word processing programs, for example, include a component for indexing documents as each one is created.

CHAPTER *7*

*O*VERCOMING
TEST ANXIETY

*I*f you want to see a good example of stress in action, just walk into a college classroom the day of a major exam. As students file in and take their seats, you can study a variety of behavior patterns for dealing with stress. One student might be nervously tapping a pencil and staring off into space. Another will be hurriedly scanning handwritten notes one last time. Others will be throwing questions at one another in a kind of oral drill, while a few will be looking over their textbooks in what may be their first reading. A few calm souls might even be nonchalantly discussing the latest "Friday the 13th" movie.

Behavior may vary but, for most students, exams are among the greatest sources of stress in college. After all, any time you take a test, something bad can happen. The worst possibility, of course, is that you will fail. Failing this particular test might lead to failing the course, you tell yourself, and failing the course could lead to academic probation and eventually to flunking out of school altogether.

Of course, failure is a relative thing, and for most students it's not just the either-or situation of passing or flunking a test that leads to stress. If that were true, only students on the academic borderline would worry about exams, and the "better" students would remain totally unruffled by the testing process. But higher achievers never seem content with just passing; they want A's or B's whenever possible, and often expend more energy worrying about exams than those who care only about avoiding failure.

The result is that tests produce a high level of anxiety in most college students. But you can reduce anxieties by taking a careful look at the exam process and by playing it smart in preparing for and taking tests. Following are several strategies anyone can follow to perform better in exams and reduce the stress involved.

Become Comfortable with Course Material

The smartest approach for avoiding test anxiety is knowing the material that has been covered to date in the course. Conversely, you can virtually guarantee problems by going into a major exam unprepared.

"The surest way to stimulate test anxiety is not to prepare," says Dr. David Frew, a professor of organizational behavior at Gannon University in Pennsylvania. "To have a reasonable shot at doing well, you need to prepare adequately."

This doesn't mean memorizing every possible fact. But at the least, you should have read all the relevant material from your textbooks and have completed any major assignments (such as math problems and worksheets). You may have been able to get away with skipping much of this material in high school classes, but don't count on the same for college. Instead, make certain you feel comfortable that you have at least a working knowledge of the subject to be covered. Doing the basic assignments still does not ensure success, but it certainly tips the scales in your favor. And if you undertake an exam with the knowledge that you have prepared for it, you should be much more confident—and less anxious—than might otherwise be the case.

To make certain you have prepared adequately for any exam, take such steps as the following:

- Develop a timetable for reviewing material, allowing a specific amount of time for each chapter or each major topic you expect the exam to cover.

- Put together a checklist of information covered since your last exam, and make certain that you can recall pertinent details about each area.

- Go back through your textbook or other assigned reading and focus on all material that appears in bold type or italics, or that is emphasized in any other way. Use a wide-tipped marker to add your own highlighting, or make a brief outline based on headings and information stressed in your textbook.

- Exchange notes with a friend and see if they contain details you may have neglected to include in your own notes. Or spend some time talking with other students about information you find vague or confusing.

- Review definitions of terms that have been introduced in class or in assigned reading.

- Go over questions or problems presented at the end of a textbook chapter or unit. If sample problems are posed, work them.

- Review the course syllabus and relate learning objectives listed there to material covered to date in the course. Chances are, anything listed in the syllabus will be given major emphasis in exams.

Play the Numbers

You can also reduce anxiety by keeping track of basic numbers and then taking advantage of them. For instance, keep tabs on your standing in each class and then calculate the minimum score you will need on any upcoming test to ensure a passing grade. This isn't possible for the first test in a class, of course, but once you begin to accumulate grades, you can then build up a cushion of "extra" points. Knowing you have this cushion will help reduce the tension related to any given exam.

It works like this. Your psychology professor has listed her grading system on the course syllabus. (Note that a syllabus is more than just a course outline; it's in effect a contract between you and the instructor, so be sure to make yourself familiar with the syllabus in every course.) The breakdown of grades is as follows:

90–100	. . . . . A
80–90	. . . . . . B
70–80	 C
60–70	. . . . . . D
under 60	. . . . F

You already have something of a break, because some grading scales are tighter. For example, 94 is the minimum for an A in some classes, as is common in high school. But a scale with 10-point intervals is more common at the college level. If each exam will carry equal weight toward the determination of the final course grade, it will be simple to calculate how well you'll have to do, test by test.

Say on the first exam you scored an 88. You may have wanted to do even better, but still you can rest easy in realizing that you've already started building up a cushion. Since 88 is 18 points above a minimum score for a passing grade (88 minus 70), you can score as low as a 52 on your next exam (70 minus 18) and still have an average of 70, a passing grade (140 divided by two).

This does *not* mean you should shoot only for a passing grade. The important point is to realize that as you build up this "bank" of extra points, the pressure is off in terms of anything really bad happening. You *will* pass the course, and you don't have to worry about failure. Each time you score above 70 on a test, the "extra" points can be added to your bank, reducing pressures during the next exam. If you're aiming for an A average, a score of 96 means you can dip to an 84 on the next test and still have an A. Whatever your performance goals, you can keep pressure down by reducing the significance of any single test.

Another way to play the numbers is to pay close attention to the relative values of individual questions on exams. Most instructors list the possible point totals along with the instructions for each portion of a written exam. If this is the case, make certain you take into account the points you can earn as you're allocating time for each answer.

For instance, a sociology exam might have 20 questions for a total possible score of 100, but each answer might not be worth five points. Instead, the first section might feature 10 true/false questions offering three points each, followed by nine short-answer question worth five points each and then one essay question worth 25 points. The first thing such a scheme should tell you is that by far the most important question is the last one, so it should be given the most time and attention. Don't dwell too much on any single question in the first part, and don't get carried away providing more information than is necessary for the short-answer questions. Instead, try to answer them reasonably quickly, so that you don't reach the essay question with only 10 minutes left in the exam period.

Since your goal when taking a test is to score the most points possible, you need to think about the exam structure as well as its content. Approach it strategically to make the best use of your strengths and minimize weaknesses, the way a baseball coach might use a left-handed pitcher against a team with mostly left-handed hitters. To ensure success and reduce your anxiety about any exam, you need to develop a game plan—including the numbers involved—and then set it in action during the relatively short time allotted for any test.

Read Exams Carefully

When a test is distributed, take your time and read each question before answering any of them. The natural tendency is to start answering the first question and then proceed from there, but you will do better by getting a sense of the whole exam.

In the first place, this will help you in planning how much attention to give to each question. At the same time, you can avoid wasting time including information for one answer that might be more appropriate for a question appearing later in the exam. In addition, your mind works on several levels, and sometimes your brain will be working on an angle to one question while you are answering another.

It's a shame to lose points on an exam by misreading a question or by failing to read instructions carefully. Take the few extra moments necessary to read everything carefully before answering, and the results are almost certain to be worth the trouble.

Stay in Control of Time

Part of the difficulty of keeping calm during exams is the fact that you are working under a time limit. That creates stress for most people. The key to overcoming that stress is to control time instead of letting it control you. Here's how:

1. *Make sure you bring a watch to any test.* Even if your classroom has a clock, there is always the possibility that it will be broken or not keep accurate time.

2. *Know how much time to devote to each portion of a test.* As soon as the exam is distributed, count the number of questions to determine how many minutes you have per question, or how many minutes per major section. Keep this calculation simple, or you will waste time instead of conserving it, but get a rough idea of your time constraints. Then monitor your progress periodically to make sure you don't spend too much time on any single question or section at the expense of others.

3. *Use any extra time constructively.* In college you can leave as soon as you've finished a test. But this relative freedom can be dangerous. Don't hurry through an exam and then leave. Use the remaining time to improve your performance. When you complete an exam under the time limit, work it to your advantage. Take whatever time is left to carefully review your answers and add improvements. For essay or short-answer tests, check your spelling, make certain you haven't left out words or important facts, and expand answers as time allows. If math problems or other figures are involved, re-check calculations. For multiple choice or other objective questions, make a small mark in the margin for any you're unsure about on first consideration, and then go back and review them after everything else has been answered. And make certain you have attempted an answer for each question! Every professor can relate depressing stories about students who accidentally skipped over questions or even whole portions of exams, torpedoing their grades in the process. A little proofreading can eliminate such problems.

Once you get in the habit of taking charge of time, you should develop greater confidence in your ability to do well in exam situations. And the more you feel in control of the situation, the less stress you will suffer.

Look at the Big Picture

If this were a perfect world, competition would not exist. And in the classroom setting, no student would strive to outperform another, with the combined efforts of the class as a whole taking priority over the status of any individual student.

The real world, of course, is different. Competition is part of the picture, and more often than not your test grades are inextricably linked to the performance of other students. Even with grade scales in effect, most professors will adjust them according to the performance of the class. For example, if you score an 86 on an exam, that will probably equate to a letter grade of B. But if all your classmates score in the 70s or below, your instructor might well adjust the grading scale, and you will earn an A instead.

What this means in terms of test strategies is simply that if you're aware of the overall class picture, you can get a better feel for your own situation and in the process reduce some of the pressure.

Try to find out what the test-score range is in each of your classes so you will have an idea of how your work compares with that of your classmates. You can do this informally by chatting with other students about their scores before or after class sessions, or by asking the instructor. Some professors list all the scores (without corresponding names) after every exam. Unless you're at the bottom of the scale, knowing the results can boost your confidence and reduce stress. It's always valuable to have a clear sense of the scores you will need to aim for on future exams to keep up with—or ahead of—the rest of the class.

Use Mnemonics

Mnemonics (from the Greek for *memory*) is just a fancy term for developing memory tricks to help you recall information. You've probably already used mnemonics in some form. Perhaps you've mastered the colors of the spectrum by memorizing Roy G. Biv (for red, orange, yellow, green, blue, indigo, and violet). Or maybe you've used the same technique to memorize the parts of math equations, lists of state capitals, or other information that must be recalled in exams.

At any rate, using memory devices is a smart way to master the kind of information that you'll be expected to provide in response to questions such as the following:

- What are five major types of national government?
- List the countries making up Latin America (or the Middle East, or the European Common Market).
- According to Carlyle, what are three symptoms of a decaying society?
- What are eight common threats to validity in statistical analysis?

You are certain to encounter questions such as these, and a system for memorizing the appropriate details will help you avoid stressful feelings during exams. The ability to recall list-type information will keep you from spending too much time straining to recall individual items, instead freeing you to spend more time on other, more complex exam questions.

You can borrow memory tricks from other sources, or you can make up your own. For example, the *New York Times* suggests you learn the following sentences if you want to remember the 14 cabinet departments of the United States, in the order they were formed: "See the dog jump in a circle. Leave her home to entertain educated veterans." Each word starts with the same letter as the department in question (State, Treasury, Defense, Justice, Interior, Agriculture, Commerce, Labor, Health and Human Services, Housing and Urban Development, Energy, Education, and Veterans Affairs).

If you're developing your own such devices, take a list and then play around with phrases or sentences that you can memorize as a key to the overall contents of the list. Let's say you want to remember the three periods of the Mesozoic Era (the Triassic, the Jurassic, and the Cretaceous). You might think of the names of three friends, Tom, John, and Carl, and use the initial letter of each as the main point. Or you might make up a silly phrase such as "try jumping creeks," where the first two letters of each word are recalled. The phrase need not make sense to anyone else, as long as it works for you. By using such techniques, you can commit various lists to memory for easy recall during exams.

Avoid Cramming

If you haven't prepared sufficiently, you might be tempted to stay up the night before an exam, trying to cram half a semester's work into a few hours. This is not, repeat *not*, a good idea!

Aside from the fact that it just doesn't work that well in terms of actual learning, cramming is one of the most stressful efforts you can undertake as a college student. It goes hand in hand with anxiety. You feel pressured from the start, realizing that you're behind, and then things only get worse as you fight the clock. Eventually it becomes not just a matter of emotional stress, but also the physical reality of tiring yourself out.

By the time you actually sit down to take the exam, you are far from your best. Instead of the calm detachment that is the ideal test-taking frame of mind, you are much more likely to be on edge and tired, which increases the probability of making careless mistakes and oversights in reading test instructions.

To avoid cramming, make certain you read the course material as it's assigned instead of delaying until exam time and tackling a huge volume of material. And don't make the common mistake of deferring work in one course to concentrate on a tougher course. That may seem like a good way to reduce stress—until you're surprised by an unexpected assignment, or you find yourself falling far behind in that "easy" course. If you read the basic material for all your classes as it is assigned rather than putting it off, you can then use the day or two before an exam to review the overall content and memorize key facts.

"It's really important to keep up with assigned material as you go along," says Kent State University professor Dr. Sue Bruning. "Just trying to cram everything in at the end usually won't do any good. Try to integrate your assignments into your daily routine instead of putting them off."

Practice Answering Questions

Familiarity does more than breed contempt—it can also build confidence. The more often you practice the art of answering questions, the better.

Have you ever watched a presidential candidate field questions from the press? No matter how tough the question, the practiced politician can provide an answer without panicking or drawing a blank. The process has been repeated so many times, it becomes a natural one. In the same way, you can benefit from frequent exposure to the challenge of answering questions. Be sure to take advantage of every opportunity to play the question-answer game that remains at the heart of the testing mechanism.

For example, if you are given a chance to retake an exam, do it. Professors sometimes give students a second shot at a test, particularly if the class as a whole has done poorly. If this happens, take advantage of the chance, even if your score was satisfactory the first time. The practice will be worth your effort.

In the same spirit, try answering questions posed in textbooks and study guides. Many texts include such questions at the end of each chapter. Answering them not only helps you become more familiar with the material covered in each chapter, but gives you valuable practice in fielding tough questions and formulating appropriate answers. You might even try establishing a time limit for any set of practice questions, so that you get used to working against the clock. That can help reduce stress in a test situation.

Take every opportunity to respond to written questions, even if the format is not especially academic in nature. Many consumer magazines, for instance, offer quizzes to readers on everything from how you get along with the opposite sex to grammar grapplers or your familiarity with Central American geography. Even games such as Trivial Pursuit and Jeopardy can serve the same purpose as they increase your comfort level with answering questions and thus limit test anxiety.

Make a Game of It

Exams don't really assess everything you know about a given subject. Instead, they take a sample of what you know. Who hasn't studied conscientiously for a test, only to find that the exam covered a handful of obscure, minor points that hadn't seemed important? If only the instructor had focused on the items you had mastered, your score would have been much higher.

Whereas acquiring knowledge is a serious, lifelong activity, testing it is, in a sense, a game. So why not approach it that way? After all, taking exams can be compared to completing a crossword puzzle or playing a board game. So instead of regarding an exam as a life-or-death situation, think of it as a challenge to your skills in playing the serious but intriguing game of succeeding in college. Here are several mental games you can play to reduce the pressure of the exam process:

1. *Me versus the Professor.* If you like competition, try this game. To prepare, eliminate everything from your mind that applies to course grades, quality points, and other stressful considerations. Instead, just approach the exam as a one-on-one contest between yourself and the professor who developed the test.

This can be fun, especially if you like the role of underdog. OK, so maybe the professor has a doctorate in the subject and years of experience in teaching. But you have the advantage of youth and energy. You are fresh and ready to have a go at that test.

In playing this game, pretend that each question is diabolically designed to lead you toward an incorrect answer. Thus every correct answer is a moral victory. Try thinking of it as a contest rather than a test, and you may even enjoy the challenge.

2. *Me against the Other Students.* Here, your competition is not the instructor but the other students in the same class. Your goal is not necessarily to outperform them academically, although that can be one way to play this game. Instead, try to rise above the tension of the exam situation by distinguishing your own calm self from the other basket cases in the class.

An aloof, superior, disdainful viewpoint is necessary for this strategy to work. It's as though you're Napoleon and the other students are mere peasants or foot soldiers in your glorious army. Or you're "Star Trek's" Spock competing with the Three Stooges for a spot on "College Bowl."

One warning here: in playing this game, keep your thoughts

to yourself. What may be a game to you could be terribly insulting to everyone else—and getting thrown out a classroom window is one form of stress you can do without!

3. *The Out-of-Body Experience.* Instead of cramming during the last few minutes before a test, take time to look around the room and study everyone as they try to cope with the situation. You can even include yourself in this exercise, taking a detached look at yourself as though through someone else's eyes.

As you notice how each person reacts to the situation, worries about your own performance can be pushed into the background. The entire exam can be viewed as some kind of experiment in parapsychology, and you're the emotionless student of humanity, observing group behavior like some invisible specter.

4. *The Old Coin Trick.* This is a variation of the out-of-body experience. Here, you use a coin to make all your worries disappear.

For this one to work, you must obtain a coin that is at least 125 years old. It need not be valuable; you can find old French and English coins at flea markets and coin shows for only a quarter or so.

Once you find one, carry it in your pocket or purse on any exam day. Before you begin your test, take out the coin and look at the date. Then think to yourself that everyone alive when that coin was minted is dead today! Whether they passed tests in some English private school or failed them miserably, *it doesn't matter.* There's nothing like mortality to put a little perspective on things.

If none of these games appeals to you, try making up your own version. The idea is to take things a little less seriously, reducing the probability of becoming overly anxious about the exam process. But you might want to keep your system to yourself so you won't have to explain it to skeptical friends.

Adapt to Different Exam Formats

One of the harsher realities of college life is that you must survive a variety of exam formats. Examination content and approach are generally left up to the instructor of each course, and each professor is likely to develop tests according to his or her own particular preferences. One may use nothing but multiple-choice exams, which from the instructor's viewpoint are usually the easiest to grade, and are especially efficient for classes with large student enrollments. Another might prefer essay questions, which are much more time consuming to grade but in many ways are more challenging to students. Others like to use true/false questions, short-answer formats, problems involving calculations and numerical answers, or combinations.

To reduce your anxiety and increase your chances of success, try to find out in advance which format a given test will employ and then prepare accordingly. Many professors refuse to discuss the content of upcoming exams, other than giving some broad guidelines about the general information to be covered. But almost all of them will tell you what format the exam will follow.

Salisbury State's Dr. Sharon Rubin gives the following advice. "Ask many questions about an examination ahead of time so you will know what to expect in a very specific way. Students tend to concentrate on content, but they don't ask enough questions about process."

For an essay exam, for instance, Rubin suggests asking questions such as: How important will general evidence be, and how much importance will be placed on specific evidence? How important is organization? Does the professor expect citations? In a 45-minute essay, how much time should be allotted for planning and outlining the argument to be used, and how much time for writing?

"Students panic less when they know what to expect," Rubin says. "Find out as much as you can about what you will encounter, and anxiety will be less of a problem."

Surviving Final Exams

The same strategies that apply to other exams should serve you well when you hit that most stressful of times, final-exam week. In addition, keep in mind that the importance of final examinations is often overrated.

Certainly final exams are important, but they represent only a portion of the grade in most courses. In fact, many professors attach no more importance to a final examination than to any other test you have already taken. Naturally you want to do well, but in such cases you can get through the experience more easily if you realize that the future of the world is not at stake.

For those classes where the final is a comprehensive one or where the score will constitute a major percentage of your course grade, prepare as much as possible ahead of time instead of waiting until the last minute. Most professors outline this kind of information in the course syllabus distributed during the first week of class, so a comprehensive exam should come as no surprise. If you know a great deal will be riding on such a test, start reading and reviewing important material several weeks before the end of the term, or quarter, and not just the night before the test. If you prepare adequately, the final exam should be no more stressful than most other tests.

Finally, keep in mind that although finals are tough, students survive them all the time. By preparing adequately and following smart test-taking strategies, you too can come through the experience with flying colors.

CHAPTER 8

*H*ANDLING THE PRESSURES OF WRITING PAPERS

*D*o you like to write research papers, reports, and other papers? If so, don't admit it too freely, or many of your classmates might think you're a bit on the weird side. After all, most students find the process of writing papers about as exciting as watching reruns of the old Lawrence Welk show.

The fact is, though, it really doesn't matter whether you enjoy writing papers or dread it more than the latest infectious disease. As a college student, you *will* be required to write papers in a variety of classes. The one "biggie" you can count on will be your second semester freshman English class, where a full-blown research paper is a standard requirement at most colleges. In addition, many other classes feature at least one paper along with other course requirements. Most

literature courses include a critical paper as a key requirement, as do many courses in history, sociology, and other
disciplines in the social sciences.

Is this just one more way for faculty members to squeeze
in a little extra torture? No, most instructors who assign papers are convinced that the process of gathering and organizing
information in a prescribed format is an extremely valuable
one. Sure, grading papers is not as much trouble as writing
them, but it's a close second. If you think about it from the
instructor's viewpoint, reading through stacks of term papers
is a lot less desirable than grading a multiple choice exam, but
professors who choose this option see real benefit to student
growth or they would not go to all that trouble.

Because they play such an important role in many
courses, papers can make or break your chances of success.
At the same time, the depth of work involved can prove more
imposing than most other assignments. Many students experience trouble in developing and completing papers, feeling
stressed in the process.

In some ways, writing papers can be even more stressful
than taking exams. After all, for most exams the pressure
builds up and then is relieved relatively quickly, as the actual
experience of answering test questions is completed in a couple of hours or less. But most papers cover a much longer time
span. Often they are assigned weeks ahead of the actual due
date, giving you plenty of time to accomplish the task but also
setting up the same time span for you to worry about it.

How to Avoid Paper Panic

Sometimes it seems as though professors live and work
in a strange vacuum. Even though you may be taking four or
five other courses at the same time, the typical professor is
only concerned with your role as a student in his or her
course. English instructors, convinced that effective writing

and research skills are essential, assign long, complicated research papers. History or sociology professors or other faculty, not content to toss off chapter after chapter of reading assignments, act as though you have nothing else to do besides spend your remaining time writing comprehensive papers for their courses. Even if you have a heavy work load from other classes, it doesn't matter.

The best defense, it is often said, is a good offense. Defend yourself against the onslaught of work dished out by your professors by attacking each paper assignment and setting up a schedule for completing the various portions of the task.

"You can develop a fighting chance by working back from deadlines," notes Dr. Sharon Rubin of Salisbury State University. "If a paper is due on a particular date, when would the first draft have to be done? When would the research have to be done? When would the library work to begin the research need to be done? When would selection of a topic need to be done? These periods of time won't be the same for everyone, but if you set your own deadlines and then work back from them, you can get a realistic perspective on when to start."

Don't use what has been called defensive avoidance, where you cope with the situation by avoiding the work at hand. Many students fall into this trap and put off researching and writing their papers until the last minute, and then begin when it's nearly impossible to do a complete and effective job. The end result? Paper panic—one of the most deviously threatening disorders on the college scene—can set in.

What Professors Look for in Assigned Papers

The big question is, What do college professors look for when they sit down to grade a stack of student papers? What will make your paper look better than the one just before it or just after?

In the first place, the quality of your thinking—and your writing—must be good. It's not enough simply to commit 1,000 words to paper just because that's the length assigned. Weak academic writing can lead to lack of enthusiasm for your work at best and a poor or failing grade at worst.

This is not to say you must write like a textbook author to succeed in college. But by devoting attention to just a few basics, you can increase your chances for success. After all, you will be completing writing assignments whether you like it or not, so why not shoot for A's or B's instead of just scraping by?

According to James Worsham, a journalism professor at Bluefield State College in West Virginia, the key to top-notch student writing is clarity of expression.

"Students often get the wrong idea about the kind of writing they think professors want to see," he says. "Too many students fill their papers with borrowed phrasing and fancy words which, at least on the surface, have an academic character. But in truth, this is not what most instructors expect or want."

In fact, good writing is intended not to impress but to communicate. The best student writing, according to Worsham, demonstrates the following characteristics:

1. *Conciseness.* Good writing gets to the point. Each sentence is as brief as possible, and each paragraph makes only those points necessary to be understood. Even a long paper needs this quality, covering in perhaps 10 concise pages what poor writing might stretch out to 12 or 15. Whatever the actual length, it is the minimum necessary to convey the subject without unnecessary "padding."

Have you ever read a boring report or article that seems to drag on forever? If so, chances are you either did not finish reading it or completed the task with a negative impression about the material. The same is true for college professors. Material that is unnecessarily long wastes their time, and they will probably not be impressed. In fact, they will very likely ignore most of it, scanning through to find obvious errors (after all, the longer the effort, the more mistakes you'll have the "oppportunity" to commit) and eventually assigning a mediocre grade or worse.

2. *Careful organization.* Careful organization is a fundamental element of any successful paper. The organizational pattern you establish not only guides the development of material during the writing process but also determines how well the instructor will be able to follow your thoughts when reading the finished paper. The best writing of any type is targeted to a specific audience, and in the case of required papers that person is your professor. Without careful and logical organization, your reader, who is also your judge, will not understand or assess the material favorably.

One effective strategy is to reduce the material to an outline. Some professors require an outline as part of the paper assignment, but even if not required, it's a good idea to base your paper on an outline to make certain you do not overlook major organizational flaws.

3. *Lack of errors.* If you want to guarantee a low grade, be sure to make plenty of errors in spelling, punctuation, and grammar. You've heard plenty about these elements all through school, so don't be surprised at their importance in college-level writing.

When professors get together at departmental meetings and conferences, one of their most common gripes is the lack of writing ability of too many college students. They see paper after paper with what they consider appalling weaknesses in the basic fundamentals of written communication. Chief among them are sentence fragments (a group of words presented as a sentence even though it lacks a subject or verb in a grammatically complete relationship), comma splices (two sentences joined together by a comma), errors in subject-verb agreement and agreement of pronouns and their antecedents, and spelling errors.

They also decry vocabulary problems, where students use a word thinking it means one thing and yet it actually doesn't make sense in that context; and problems with punctuation (leaving out apostrophes, adding apostrophes when they are unnecessary, and so forth). From such examples you might think only English professors care about such matters, but faculty members in other disciplines get equally distraught when their students submit papers with these kinds of problems. And of course the results are not just frustrated professors but also lower grades on student papers.

You can avoid adding to this misery through careful writing that includes attention to these kinds of details. This should include as a minimum consulting reference books as you write (dictionaries, grammar and usage guides, and so forth). It is also advisable to develop more than one draft and then refine each version until all major errors are caught and corrected. If possible, it's never a bad idea to have someone else read the paper before you consider it finished. The old adage "two heads are better than one" usually holds true when you are working on a long paper. The closer you become to the material, the more likely you are to overlook an obvious error that a fresh reader will catch immediately.

How to Select a Topic

When it's time to write a paper, your subject might be assigned. If so, great. You can take the assignment and go right to work on it.

What is more likely, however, is that part of your task is to choose your topic. This sounds simple enough, but for many students selecting a topic is almost as stressful as writing the paper itself. How do you know where to begin? What if six other students write on the same subject? What does the professor really expect, anyway? These and other questions can present difficulties.

To overcome this problem, talk with other students and see what they have selected. You won't want to duplicate their efforts, but often another student's choice will trigger your own idea, which might be to take the other side of the same issue or cover it from a different angle.

Or look through reference works in the library that list periodical articles. By reviewing the types of articles that have been written about various subjects, you can get an idea of topics that need to be readdressed or covered in a different way.

If you still have problems, talk with your instructor. Most professors will be glad to share some ideas if you are struggling to identify a topic.

Basic Prewriting Strategies

One of the biggest mistakes you can make is simply to sit down and begin writing without taking some time to plan your efforts. Writing is not really a one-two-three process, at least for most people. In other words, the normal procedure is not for one sentence to lead naturally into the next, without any changes or adjustments as the total effort grows. Instead, it's more like the creation of a statue out of clay, where the artist lumps some clay together, takes some out, adds some more, and then keeps adjusting as the work progresses.

To take best advantage of the natural writing process, it's best to build some preliminary plans and then expand them, rather than just writing a beginning, middle, and end of your paper. This can be done in different ways to accommodate your own individual style, but everyone should observe several basics.

The first of these is research. This may not be necessary for short, personal essays of the type often assigned in freshman composition classes. But for longer papers and those based on anything other than your own experience, gathering information to incorporate into the paper is vital.

The word *research* may sound imposing, but it really can

be rather simple. For the kind of research needed for papers, this may just mean some reading in books or journals to obtain basic facts and background information. At the postsecondary level this will involve more than looking up the subject in an encyclopedia, but don't worry if you feel uncomfortable about negotiating a college or university library. You will probably receive instruction about using the library in your first-year English courses, but even if that is not the case library staff members will be happy to help you learn your way around.

At any rate, background research provides a couple of important benefits to your writing efforts. Most important, it increases your own knowledge of whatever subject is being addressed. Unless you happen to be the world's greatest authority on the subject, facts and opinions developed by other writers are essential to help you understand the topic and say enough about it to build a strong paper. Such material also provides citations which can be built into the paper, a standard requirement in most academic writing.

Today's students have one tremendous advantage over those of previous generations: the computer. By using computer search services, computerized library holdings, and similar features of modern college libraries, you can avoid much of the boring labor that once nagged college students as they wandered through dark library basements trying to find dusty books or back issues of obscure periodicals.

Once you conduct some research efforts, the next step will be to organize your information. Probably the best tool for such organization is an outline. Some students hate to develop outlines, but they can provide a great way of planning each section of your paper. An outline does not need to follow the rigid format requirements you may have struggled with in high school. Instead, it can simply be a list of subject headings and the order in which you plan to address them, or it can follow any other format you might prefer.

As you think ahead, you might also write different portions of the paper as ideas occur to you. For example, a passage that might appear in the middle of the paper can be written first while you are researching that section, or the introduction can be written well ahead of time to help clarify your own approach to the subject.

Writing Reports

In addition to formal research papers or term papers, class reports can be developed for a variety of purposes. These can include summaries of special projects, bibliographical reports, and laboratory studies, among others. Their basic purpose is to present information that supplements textbook material.

Reports can benefit from the same basic principles that apply to formal papers and other student writing. In particular, they require careful organization so that all material provided is readily understandable to the instructor.

Longer reports can be organized in the following pattern:

Title page

Abstract (brief summary)

Introduction

Table of contents

Body of the report

Illustrations and figures

Conclusions

Appendix

Some of these elements, such as an abstract and a table of contents, can be skipped for shorter reports. An appendix is optional regardless of length; it can be helpful for adding detailed information (such as raw data, samples of forms or extra tables) that would bog down the body of the report itself.

Keeping Your Writing Clear

Improving writing can be a complex process. After all, even professional writers face the task of continually polishing their work. And when they believe it's perfect, the next step involves turning the material over to editors who then proceed to add their own improvements. But many elements of writing are relatively uncomplicated and can be mastered by any student. Here are several steps you can take to improve the clarity of academic papers.

1. *Cut out unnecessary words.* Spoken language tends to be filled with redundancies and an overall lack of precision. This is rarely a problem, since we can clarify and correct things as we speak. But written language, which must stand on its own without amplification, has to be more precise and less cumbersome.

Eliminating unneeded words is one way to simplify and improve writing. For example, changing the phrase "blue in color" to just "blue" will enhance readability. Since blue *is* a color, the rest of the phrase is not needed. In the same way, trim phrases such as "round in shape" to "round," "in the year 1865" to "in 1865," "each and every" to just "each" or "every," and "consensus of opinion" to simply "consensus."

Similarly, instead of phrases such as "the dean made a recommendation, and "Congress granted authorization", write "the dean recommended" and "Congress authorized." For "the books that are outdated," substitute "outdated books." Remember, in the student writing game, more is not better. Whenever possible, eliminate words that do not really add to your intended meaning.

2. *Use simple words.* Words don't just pop out of the air; you choose them, consciously or not, from your working vocabulary. If the aim is really to communicate, why make things confusing by selecting big words when small ones will do?

Professors are often guilty of this, but they are seldom impressed by student efforts to do the same. In fact, using words that aren't familiar to you can be dangerous, because the chances for misusing them may be high. A much safer route is to use simple, ordinary language. Your thoughts can be important without being shrouded in the mysteries of an artificially complicated vocabulary.

For instance, never write "facilitate" when "help" will convey the same idea. Use "start" instead of "commence" or "initiate," "happen" rather than "transpire," and "use" instead of "utilize."

3. *Keep sentences short.* Long sentences pose special dangers. You have a greater chance of making a serious grammatical error, because too many elements must be properly coordinated. And even if the passage is technically correct, your instructor is likely to become confused or miss key details owing to the sheer length of the sentence.

In general, sentences of fewer than 30 words are preferred. Some may be longer for the sake of variety, but a reliance on shorter sentences will support the overall goal of clear communication.

4. *Avoid repetition of words.* Variety is an important element in written work. Repeating the same word several times in a sentence or paragraph can be a real annoyance, in the process detracting from the overall impact of any written passage.

This is easy to avoid with a little care. Just use synonyms to provide some variety. For example, in a paper about the invention of the computer, you can refer to the "computer," "device," "machine," or "unit," interspersing these labels as needed. If you have trouble thinking of alternative phrasing, consult a dictionary or thesaurus.

5. *Avoid the common pitfalls of padding, an unclear topic, and mechanical errors.*

—*Padding.* For some reason, students tend to think that longer papers will somehow impress professors more than short ones. But the real truth is that conciseness is just as important in papers and reports as in short compositions and other written works. Don't make the mistake of padding your papers with unnecessary material. A 30-page paper is *not* better than a 10-page effort, if you can cover all the material in 10 pages (and if the assignment doesn't specify a greater length). Professors are impressed by substance. They don't grade papers by the pound! In fact, the more material presented, the less likely your major points will be read and understood.

—*An unclear topic.* Just what is the main point of your paper? This may not be as clear as you think. Many papers suffer from the lack of a single main idea.

To avoid confusion, state your main idea in clear terms at the beginning of the paper and again at the end. Remember, your professor will be carefully evaluating your efforts, and the major point you are trying to make should be easily identifiable.

—*Mechanical errors.* It naturally takes longer to develop, type, and edit a complex paper than a short composition. And thanks to the sheer volume involved, longer papers are especially vulnerable to spelling errors, grammatical blunders, and awkward phrasing.

Never consider a paper completed until you have checked it thoroughly for such errors. It can be tempting to get rid of any project that has taken hours (or days or weeks!) to finish, but hasty action at the end can result in sloppy work.

Ideally, you should set the paper aside and then return to it a day or two later for final editing, when you can examine the work with a fresh eye. If this is not possible, at least read it two or three times before turning it over to your professor.

CHAPTER *9*

*W*HAT TO DO
WHEN THE FOCUS
IS ON YOU

*I*t's like a scene from a Stephen King movie: distorted faces surround you, and your heart thunders against your chest as the mounting fear paralyzes your entire body. No, the situation is not an aborted escape from some unearthly monster. But it's the next worst thing, as you take your dreaded turn delivering a speech in your freshman English class or Introduction to Public Speaking.

OK, so maybe the situation is not really that bad. But one of life's greatest fears, at least for some people, is speaking before a group. And even if you hate public speaking, that will not keep you from suffering through this experience. Sooner or later, every college student will face the task of making oral reports, speeches, or other presentations. In addition, there will be times when the focus is on you as you meet individually with professors or administrators.

Although this might sound imposing, you can manage it by observing some basic considerations in communicating orally. Following are some tips for making the most of this often stressful challenge.

Volunteer to Go First

What, are you crazy? That may be your initial reaction to such a suggestion, especially if speaking before a group is something you dread. But there is much to be said for taking the first shot at an oral presentation. The main advantage is that you get through the experience quickly, instead of sweating it out while other students take their turns. Sure, it's not easy to stand up as the lead-off speaker, but things are not going to get any easier as you wait. To the contrary, the pressure tends to mount as it nears time for your presentation, and the uncomfortable feelings are prolonged. Even worse, only so many students can give talks during any single class meeting, so you can find yourself preparing in advance and then nervously waiting your turn once class begins, only to have the class period end before getting your chance. So you end up having to go through the same nerve-racking process again.

Another advantage is that your performance is judged on its own merits instead of in comparison to those of other students. The phrase "tough act to follow" can develop real meaning if you're unlucky enough to follow a student who is a pro at public speaking.

Finally, if you do take the "get it over with" approach, after the job is accomplished you can sit back and enjoy listening to everyone else's speeches instead of dwelling on your own preparations.

126

Narrow Down Your Topic

Whether your topic is assigned or one you select, make sure it is something that can be adequately covered in a short time. If you make the mistake of failing to focus on some specific aspect of the broader topic, your chances of delivering a good talk are next to impossible.

For example, don't try to speak on the Civil War, a subject that fills volumes and volumes of books and one that could never be adequately addressed in just a few minutes. It would be much better to limit your subject to the everyday camp life of a Confederate private, the battle between the *Monitor* and the *Merrimac*, how the draft worked during the Civil War, common misconceptions about slavery, or some similarly well-defined topic. Just as in a written composition, the less material you attempt to cover, the better. This way you are more likely to provide specific information that will genuinely interest an audience, rather than a broad overview of something your listeners may already know.

Think of Yourself as an Expert

Once you gather some information about a subject, chances are you will know more about it than most members of any given audience. In a sense, you become an expert on the topic, at least in comparison to other members of a class. Remember, they're just students too, and if you delve into virtually any subject, you can acquire enough information to make an oral presentation that will provide facts everyone in the class does not possess. This really goes hand in hand with selecting a sufficiently narrow topic, for the more specialized your topic, the less likely anyone else in the audience will know much about it.

You can say the same thing about your professors, but with less certainty. If you pick some obscure topic about the Incas, your history professor might just happen to be a genuine expert. Maybe she completed her doctoral research on the very same topic. In that case, you'd better know your stuff! To be safe on this point, discuss your topic with the instructor in advance of actually preparing the talk, and try to stay away from subjects on which the professor is an authority or that cannot be mastered sufficiently for your efforts to hold up under the scrutiny of someone who really knows the subject.

Prepare Yourself

Whenever you know you will be speaking before a group, take the time to prepare yourself adequately. If you're well prepared your confidence level is bound to improve, and with confidence comes good performance.

First, sketch out a brief outline of the points you plan to cover. This need not be a formal document but rather a personalized outline that helps you organize the presentation. An outline of this type doesn't have to be neat, written in complete sentences, or even readable to anyone else, as long as you can make sense of it.

Next, do some research to obtain a few interesting facts about the subject. It's best to consult several sources as opposed to limiting yourself to just one, but in any case make certain you back up your own knowledge with authoritative sources.

After you have fleshed out the outline, practice the presentation at least three times. Reading over your notes silently is not enough; you have to run through the speech *out loud* to get a real feel for the material and how it will work as an oral presentation. Skipping this preliminary stage is like entering a skydiving competition after you have read books on the subject but have never actually jumped from an airplane!

After polishing your mastery of the wording, stand in front of a mirror and practice taking control of the visual side of the presentation. Be alert for distracting habits such as shuffling your feet, waving your hands excessively, playing with your hair, and other signs of nervousness. If you can videotape a practice session, so much the better. Viewing yourself as others see you will provide insights into needed improvements in your style of delivery.

In addition, make certain you know your material well enough that you can talk comfortably without depending too much on notes. And at all costs, stay away from the deathly boring practice of reading to your audience. Instead, prepare yourself to *talk* to them in a calm, confident manner.

Adapt to Your Audience

The best speakers always adjust their presentations according to the level and background of the audience. Experienced politicians tend to be masters at this kind of adaptation. A senator's speech to a group of farmers may employ an entirely different style and approach than a presentation to corporation executives, or then again to a ladies' garden club. In fact, it may be hard to believe the speaker at these different events is even the same person.

Although in college the range of possibilities is generally smaller, it's still important to adapt your material to the group who will be listening. For example, say you're giving a talk on searching for comets with a reflecting telescope. If this is in freshman English or your public speaking class, you will need to select nontechnical terms and take time to explain concepts that may be unfamiliar to a general audience. On the other hand, if the talk is for the astronomy club, your vocabulary can be much more technical.

For in-class presentations, keep in mind that you actually have a dual audience: the other students and the instructor. If the presentation is being made as a class assignment, the assessment of the instructor will be more important than that of all the students combined, so be sure to present material in a way that will favorably impress the professor.

Grab Your Audience's Attention

If possible, think of some way to spark the interest of your listeners at the very start of your presentation. If you can accomplish this early, the audience will be more receptive to points you make later. At the same time, getting off to a good start boosts your confidence and improves your overall level of performance.

One way to demand attention is to use an audiovisual aid. This can be a chart, a photograph, or an actual object related to the subject of your presentation. For instance, a talk on military aircraft might be accompanied by slides or photos of airplanes, or even a plastic scale model.

Sometimes, daring or off-the-wall strategies will work here when they might otherwise flop. I once saw a student begin a speech by taking out some gunpowder and lighting a match to it. That certainly got everyone's attention! He then proceeded to explain that gunpowder is explosive only when confined and went on to give his talk about how to prepare your own rifle ammunition.

If you use printed materials, don't make the mistake of handing them out to your audience before the presentation or while you're speaking. Given this opportunity, people will invariably read the handouts instead of listening to what you're saying, and you will lose a good portion of their attention. Handouts are fine, but distribute them at the end of your presentation, not before.

Make Eye Contact

When addressing a group, you should be talking *to* people, not *at* them. In other words, individuals in your audience should feel you are speaking directly to them, not just flinging information in their general direction without caring whether they absorb it.

I once had a literature professor who never looked directly at anyone while he was lecturing. Instead, he just stood there reading from his notes, and whenever he looked up he stared at a point high on the back wall of the classroom. This concerted effort to avoid eye contact was unnerving, and it was no surprise that students found the class completely boring. One student even made a habit of reading the newspaper during class, as if daring the professor to notice him. But the professor didn't react (or pretended not to notice), and class went on uninterrupted in its dull, ineffective style.

The fact is, people need to feel involved if an oral presentation is to be successful. By making eye contact with members of your audience, you establish a kind of link with each of them, boosting their interest level as a result.

Speak Up

A common weakness of inexperienced speakers is that they speak too softly and the audience must strain to hear them. If you're nervous or you simply have a relatively soft voice, all the positive qualities of your presentation could be canceled out by this single weakness. If people can't hear you, there is no way your efforts will be a success.

The main tool for counteracting this problem is awareness. If you realize that your voice level is too low, all you have to do is speak more loudly! This sounds simple enough, but if you're very nervous it's possible to be so clouded with fear that you don't even realize your voice is inaudible. To avoid the problem in the first place, practice speaking aloud *before* the actual presentation. Give your speech alone in your dorm room, or ask several friends to listen. Or speak into a tape recorder and then play the speech back to pick up on this problem.

In addition, be aware during the actual talk of any problems in people hearing you. You can tell if your audience is having difficulty in hearing just by watching their faces. Force yourself to speak up if this occurs, even if you find it difficult.

Make Sure Your Facts Are Accurate

If you use numbers, dates, or other facts in an oral presentation, be sure to check out their accuracy before including them. An incorrect fact or figure can prove devastating to the overall effectiveness of a presentation, especially if someone in the audience challenges it.

Make certain any sources you use are reputable. The *New York Times* is a reputable source; the *National Enquirer* is not. If you're uncertain about any source, check with your instructor before using it.

Control the Speed of the Presentation

Sometimes speaking before a group seems like an experience out of the Twilight Zone. Time seems to slow down, and the minutes drag on like hours. You labor through the presentation and conclude, only to find out you've talked for only three minutes, when the instructor had asked for at least 10.

On the other hand, you may have carefully prepared your material, but as you present it you lose track of the time, and what had been intended as a short talk ends up taking more than 20 minutes.

In either of these cases, your effectiveness will have been greatly limited. Staying within an established time frame is vital to successful oral presentations. To avoid this problem, place a watch beside your notes on the lectern or desk, and consult it unobtrusively but frequently. Or use a clock if the classroom has one, or bring one along that you can place in the back of the room where it will be in plain sight as you speak.

Try to avoid talking too fast. If you speak rapidly, several things can happen, and all of them are bad. In addition to ending the presentation too soon, you may put yourself in a position where the audience simply can't understand you as words and sentences run together and become indistinguishable. At the same time, you will lose the appearance of calmness so important to making a good impression.

Master Pronunciation

You can be sailing along in full control of your presentation, but if you pronounce a word incorrectly the overall impact will suddenly be diminished. It's one thing to merely stumble over a word or two because of nervousness or a simple slip of the tongue which can be immediately corrected, but it's another to mispronounce one or more words just because they are not a part of your normal working vocabulary.

As you write material and practice your presentation take time to look up any words that you're not sure about, and practice saying each one five or 10 times to make certain you have it mastered. If you keep slipping on any one word, simply replace it with another.

Deliver an Effective Conclusion

One of the most dissatisfying experiences in public speaking is to cruise along for the first part of the talk, only to end with a weak conclusion that leaves little impact on the audience. Too often, students prepare heavily for the first part of the presentation, assuming that the remainder will more or less develop on its own as the talk progresses. Unfortunately, failure to plan a forceful conclusion can negate much of an otherwise positive presentation.

As you prepare for an in-class oral report or other talk, be sure to include a structured, upbeat ending. There are a number of ways to build an effective conclusion, with the main consideration being the need to control this portion of the talk rather than just letting it happen.

The most traditional type of conclusion is a summary of each major point that has just been covered. It's the old triple T formula: tell 'em what you're gonna tell 'em, tell 'em, and then tell 'em what you told 'em. Here you restate each point, taking care to use new phrasing and brief language so you won't end up repeating yourself and boring the audience. This can be especially effective for talks intended to persuade an audience, for it allows you to emphasize the primary content in such a way that your message is very clear and the audience has heard each important point at least twice. Keeping this kind of summary short is essential, though, so it won't sound as though you're talking in circles.

Variations of this strategy include restating the overall thesis instead of individual points, issuing a challenge or call to action, or winding up with a provocative statement such as a prediction of things to come. Or you can use an anecdote that illustrates your main idea.

Communicating One-on-One

Speaking before a group is not the only situation in which you want to put your best foot forward as far as communication skills are concerned. Meeting individually with a professor or other college official can be almost as imposing. But you can make this go smoothly by thinking before acting and observing basic strategies such as the following:

1. *Be punctual.* One way to get off to a lousy start in a one-on-one situation is to show up late. If a specific time has been scheduled for your meeting, be sure to make it at the appointed hour. You might not turn into a pumpkin if you're late, but you won't win any points, either.

To avoid this problem, plan to arrive at the general vicinity of the meeting place at least 10 or 15 minutes early. This doesn't mean popping in on your professor before he or she is ready, which can be an inconvenience in itself. But if you plan to arrive early in the same building, this extra few minutes can save you from being late if some delay occurs.

Even at that, something unforeseen could make you unavoidably late. If your car has a dead battery and there's no way to make it on time, call ahead and indicate that you'll be late, asking if the professor will still have time to see you on this basis.

If you find you must cancel your meeting, say so as far in advance as possible. Canceling will never endear you to others, but it should not be a problem if you cite a legitimate reason, and if you don't wait until the last minute to inform the other party.

2. *Show interest in the session.* A key to any successful interaction is showing interest in the matter being discussed. Just as with a presentation before a group, it is important to maintain good eye contact. When you are talking, take every opportunity to look the person straight in the eye. As appropriate,

nod your head or respond verbally. Avoid looking down at your feet or writing notes without looking up.

Don't just listen, but also contribute your own thoughts. And never hesitate to ask questions if you're not absolutely clear about what's been said. Professors and administrators are accustomed to fielding questions and seldom mind giving you a straight answer as long as you are polite.

3. *Be yourself.* Honesty, they say, is always the best policy. And the most honest approach of all is simply to be yourself. Don't pretend that you understand more than you do, and don't adopt a stiff, formal way of speaking if that's not the real you. Sometimes in dealing with faculty members, students try to sound like professors themselves, spicing up their vocabulary with five-syllable words or eliminating any hint of humor or personality. But few faculty are impressed by such efforts.

Remember that flattery can be deadly. Some professors may enjoy hearing that their lecture was the most enthralling experience you've had in weeks, but others won't buy it. In fact, flattery that seems insincere will damage rather than enhance your standing.

4. *Don't be too aggressive.* Although it's important to demonstrate a vigorous personality, don't make the mistake of coming across as too aggressive. Never forget that the professor or administrator is the one in charge, *not* you.

So let the other person control things by setting the pace of the discussion, signaling when he or she thinks you've used up your time, or interrupting the session to take a phone call or to respond if someone else drops into the office.

5. *Get things in writing.* Often, student meetings with professors or administrators are based on a special request of the student. You might be asking to substitute one course for another, or to drop or add a course, or to exceed the normal limit on academic loads. If that is the case, you can save yourself some future stress by getting a confirmation of any resultant agreement *in writing*. Experienced students too often relate all kinds of frightening stories about obtaining oral

approval for some important matter in a one-on-one session with a college official, only to be challenged later by someone else on the same point. Maybe the official or professor simply forgot the conversation. Or perhaps your case was confused with that of another student. Whatever the excuse, you might find yourself in real trouble if you can't verify the appropriate decision in writing.

For example, take the case of the request for a course substitution. Say the Fine Arts Survey is a required course in your degree program, but you've already covered much of that material through a special arts program you completed the summer after your senior year in high school. You would rather take a course on European novels, and you successfully build a case that convinces the dean to agree to a course substitution. No problem, she says, and you go ahead and take European Novels. A year later, however, an adviser insists that you enroll in Fine Arts Survey. You try to explain the course substitution but are told no record of an approval can be found in your file, or anywhere else, for that matter. You go back to talk to the dean but find she is no longer employed at this college. Without any proof, you end up having to take the survey course and in essence wasting the European novels class, for you didn't have any room for an elective even though you completed it successfully.

The solution? Don't let this happen in the first place. Get a signature on the spot, and keep it where you can find it later. Most colleges and universities have scores of different forms, and all you must do is get the right one filled out and then keep it where you can find it.

All this may sound bureaucratic, and it is! But operating in this way will help you avoid headaches, heartaches, and undue stress whenever you must back up what you say with written documentation.

CHAPTER 10

*T*HE PHYSICAL SIDE OF COUNTERACTING STRESS

A long with psychological and emotional factors, keep in mind that other considerations such as exercise and diet play an important role in any efforts to counteract the negative effects of stress. Stress management is not just an emotional matter, but also a physical one.

Fighting Stress with Exercise

Visit any university campus, and you will see students at both ends of the exercise spectrum. Early in the morning or late in the evening, you'll spot joggers working their way across campus streets. On sunny afternoons there will be groups of students playing volleyball or softball, pairs tossing frisbees, and people involved in a variety of other sports and games.

At the other extreme can be found students whose most strenuous exercise for the day consists of lifting 10 pounds of textbooks or making 5,000 keystrokes on a computer keyboard. Their minds may be active, but their bodies are shot! Or if not yet "shot," the patterns that will lead in that direction are being developed.

The problem here often goes back to the change in routine that college brings for many students. Say you played on your high school basketball team, but like 95 percent of all high school players you really didn't have the skills to play ball at the intercollegiate level. So instead of running countless trips up and down the court every week, you save your efforts for an occasional pickup game and spend more time eating and studying than anything else.

If you fit into the first category as one who exercises regularly, that's great. If not, it's time to reassess your situation. After all, a good exercise program can do wonders to overcome negative effects of stress.

"Some kind of physical activity should definitely be a part of any college student's routine," says Georgia State University's John Krafka. "Exercise provides a break from the mental strain, and helps you ward off stress-related problems."

Not only will exercise increase your stamina and overall well-being, but strenuous activity can itself be a great stress fighter. Slamming a tennis ball across the net, working out on a rowing machine, or engaging in other hard exercise helps release pent-up frustrations or other emotions. At the same time, rigorous activity causes the body to produce neurochemicals called endorphins, which can help counter stress and provide a keen sense of pleasure and, under the right conditions, even the euphoria called "exercise high."

When you first think of exercise, you might envision unpleasant calisthenics: half killing yourself with endless repetitions of jumping jacks or push-ups or other merciless attacks on your body. But all kinds of highly enjoyable physical activities will provide just as much good without making you feel as if you've just joined the Army.

As far as stress control is concerned, probably the best form of physical activity is *aerobic* exercise. Everyone has heard of aerobics, but you might not realize that a variety of activities can provide aerobic benefits. Aerobic exercises are those that speed up your heart rate, breathing, and related functions over a long enough period (usually at least 20 minutes) to substantially increase the body's use of oxygen. Running a 100-meter dash is not an aerobic exercise, but jogging three miles is. Swimming, bicycling, skating, and dancing are also aerobic activities.

Even walking can provide aerobic benefits, and if you're not exercising regularly this might be the best place to start. As the world's oldest form of transportation, walking seems to have been rediscovered in recent years as one of the best forms of exercise available. Walking has all kinds of advantages. It is easy, requiring no special athletic ability. Virtually anyone other than those with certain physical handicaps can benefit.

Walking is also cheap. There is no need for special equipment, except perhaps a pair of walking shoes if you really plan to put in the miles. Everything else is free, in contrast to many other sports such as golf, bowling, and other activities that can be fairly expensive. You can walk virtually anywhere, whether you attend an urban university in a large, congested city, or a rural college sprawling across acres of open land.

Running and jogging offer the same level of convenience, with the added benefit that they tax the body even more than walking. Or if you think those activities are boring, you might want to try swimming or bicycling.

If you enjoy competition or just companionship, team sports provide an entirely different exercise option. Even if you are not the type of superb athlete who will flourish in the high-performance world of intercollegiate competition, that does not rule out team sports. You can participate in the fun and challenge of team competition in a variety of ways.

Most colleges offer intramural sports programs to provide such an outlet. Intramural teams are made up of students from within a single institution and are designed for fun rather than the intense competition of games between colleges and universities. Not only is there no requirement that you be a great athlete to participate, you really don't even need to be a good one.

At Virginia Commonwealth University in Richmond, Virginia, for example, a variety of intramural sports operate in leagues for men, women, and coeducational teams. These include team sports such as softball, basketball, and flag football, along with more unusual activities such as inner-tube water polo, pickleball, wallyball, and five-kilometer runs.

These intramural sports are supplemented by a number of club sports, which are recognized by the university but operate more independently. They include men's lacrosse, women's soccer, men's rugby, weight lifting, judo, karate, fencing, scuba diving, and swimming.

If you want to combine exercise with getting away from it all, you might consider special outdoor adventure programs sponsored by some universities. At Virginia Commonwealth, students can sign up for white-water rafting excursions, camping trips, canoeing expeditions, caving, backpacking trips, cross-country skiing trips, bicycle trips, and other challenging activities. Extra fees are involved, but they include any special equipment needed, and many outings are designed for beginners.

Georgia State University sponsors a Challenge Adventure program, where students spend a day in "the great outdoors" tackling an unusual ropes course. This consists of a series of challenges such as scaling a 14-foot wall on your own and climbing as high as 25 feet in a group challenge course. The adventure not only provides exercise but builds confidence and trust levels.

"Many institutions provide outlets such as these," notes John Krafka, "or at least sponsor less unusual outings such as skiing and hiking. If you get a chance to try something like this, it can be a great outlet."

Paying Attention to Your Diet

College students are notorious for their often creative diets. Cold pizza for breakfast, potato chips and cookies for lunch, and other nontraditional menus are too often the norm. Of course most colleges provide meal plans through cafeterias, but many students either skip what they consider second-rate institutional meals or supplement cafeteria food with frequent trips to fast food restaurants or private stocks of junk food stashed in dorm rooms or apartments. After all, Mom or Dad isn't there anymore to insist that you eat your vegetables or to nag you for making your third trip of the night to the refrigerator!

Aside from its basic role in your physical health, a good diet is an important element of an antistress lifestyle. Too often, students respond to stress by overeating, drinking too much, or smoking—all of which affect health negatively. Obviously, it's important to avoid such behaviors.

"College students are adults, and they can't be forced to eat nutritiously," Salisbury State's Dr. Sharon Rubin says. "But we all know that good diet and regular exercise are very important in maintaining perspective and positive feelings."

If you're already eating properly, keep it up. If not, why not start paying more attention to this important aspect of good health? The old saying "you are what you eat" may not be original, but there is a lot of truth to it.

Taking Time to Enjoy Life

To succeed as a college student, you will have to work hard. Unless you have a photographic memory or other intellectual gifts that allow you to breeze through your classes, your chances of success will be directly related, at least in part, to how hard you are willing to work. And when you think about it, isn't this part of the value system you've been taught since childhood? If you study diligently, work hard, and plan for the future, success and happiness await you, according to this philosophy.

At the same time, everyone needs to take it easy sometimes. And this includes you!

Students too often feel guilty if they're not reading an assignment, studying for an exam, working on a paper, or otherwise doing some kind of academic work. But it's really not a smart idea to spend *all* your time in such activities. In fact, virtually every day you spend in college should include some leisure time.

Take time out to participate in extracurricular activities. Whether this means academic clubs, intramural sports, playing a musical instrument, or some other activity, don't allow yourself to become caught in the academic grind where everything revolves around performance.

Of course, too many social activities, when combined with your academic work, can be as stressful as too much studying alone. Some students fall into the trap of trying to fit a little bit of everything into their lives, almost as though it's some kind of contest. Keeping perpetually busy can be a kind of status game, where the one who maintains the most hectic schedule wins.

If you want to avoid stress problems, don't play this game. Although it's a good idea to join campus organizations or find other social outlets, don't overdo things. Participate in some activities you truly enjoy, but at the same time hold back from some opportunities. Otherwise, college life may become a whirlwind schedule of commitments and obligations.

In contrast to organized activities, one of the best ways to spend some free time is to share it with others. Going for a walk or taking in a movie can be fun, but it will probably be even more enjoyable if the time is spent with some friends.

Just killing time with other students can be a relaxing change of pace from academics. In addition to the break in routine, a benefit of spending time with others is that the interaction prevents you from dwelling only on yourself. In the process of talking and sharing with others, a few minutes or hours can be doubly relaxing.

Change Your Scenery

Another avenue to relaxation is grabbing a fresh perspective on things through a change in your environment. Wouldn't it be great to forget about classes and fly to Hawaii for a couple of weeks of lounging on the beach?

OK, that's not in the cards for most of us, at least right now. But you can gain similar benefits from a weekend trip away from the campus or just an afternoon at the mall or ballpark. The important point is not where you go, but simply getting away from your everyday environment. Even a few hours away from the normal routine can be a source of renewal.

Don't Do Anything at All

Sometimes even the most wholesome of activities is the wrong strategy for relaxation. Taking a trip, for example, can be exhausting as well as enjoyable. There are times when the smartest approach is simply to do nothing at all.

Occasionally, try sitting back and listening to music without doing anything else at the same time. Or take a nap. Or give yourself the evening off with a promise of no homework. In the process, try to avoid thinking about any problems or tasks you must accomplish. Instead, treat yourself to the luxury of doing absolutely nothing.

Of course, it's essential to choose the right time to fold up in this manner. Taking Tuesday evening off might be a disaster if you have two major exams scheduled for Wednesday morning, for example. On the other hand, there are times when taking a break is the smartest thing you can do and the best gift you can give yourself.

CHAPTER *11*

*R*ELAXING TO REDUCE STRESS

T o avoid stress, just take it easy. Such simplistic advice may be fine when you're in total control of your life, but who is that lucky? When you're juggling a full load of classes, there may be no apparent escape from the pressures of academic life. You can't simply take a few weeks off when feeling stressed—at least not if you ever want to graduate!

Deep Breathing

Even at the most hectic times, you can use simple relaxation techniques to help fight stress while taking only a few

147

minutes from your daily schedule. Have you ever heard the old advice to "take a deep breath" to avoid losing control when facing anger or fear? Actually, the technique of deep breathing can provide an effective way to relieve stress.

The next time you feel pressured by an overload of homework or exam preparations, why not try a few moments of deep breathing? To get started, just break off your studies, put yourself in a comfortable sitting position, and begin taking deep, measured breaths. *Think* about the breathing process as you take each breath, feeling the new oxygen flowing into your body and giving you a fresh start on things. If you prefer, count each breath, until you've taken 20 or 30—or whatever number suits you best. When you finish the process and return to work, you may be surprised at how much more relaxed you feel as a result of this simple routine.

Visualization

A variation of the deep breathing exercise is to visualize some scene that you associate with relaxation. For example, close your eyes and think about the ocean surf rolling against a moonlit beach, or a quiet mountain scene where the only sounds are a few birds and the murmur of a clear mountain stream. The subject is not important, as long as it works for you (although many people find water-related scenes most effective). What matters is that you visualize the scene as graphically as possible, in the process forgetting for a few minutes about academic hassles. During the process you keep disruptive thoughts out of your mind, focusing only on this predetermined mental picture. In these brief "escapes," your body will slow down a bit from the aggressive pace that is likely to contribute to feelings of stress. Your attitude will be calmer, and you will be less vulnerable to stress-related problems. Just a few minutes of visualization can be surprisingly refreshing.

In case you can't think of a scene that you find especially relaxing, here is a sample vignette for your consideration. Read it over and if you like it, commit the scene to memory. Or develop your own version of a calm, peaceful scene. Then whenever you feel pressured, tired, or both, find a comfortable chair and make yourself at ease. Close your eyes, concentrate on the scene, and *relax*.

Sample Relaxation Scene: You are lying on your back on a large, comfortable air mattress in the middle of a pool of deep blue water. This small, secluded lake is the most dazzling feature of an immense forest, with huge trees towering over the lake on three sides. Birds flit about in the distance, adding specks of yellow, red, and other bright hues to the background.

At one end of the lake, a lovely waterfall pours a constant stream of fresh water into the lake, its distant roar drowning out any other noises that might intrude on the atmosphere of calmness and solitude. A fine mist fills the air, caressing your face and providing a cool touch to an incredibly beautiful day.

Progressive Relaxation

Another relaxation technique involves focusing on your muscles instead of an external scene, progressively "relaxing" different parts of your body to achieve a total calming effect.

To start out, you must be in a sitting or lying position. With your eyes closed, concentrate on one part of your body—say a finger or hand—and think about it becoming increasingly relaxed, the tension flowing out of each muscle. Then do the same with the next limb, progressing until your entire body has gone through the process. This technique can be quite effective once you become accustomed to it, as concentrating on the process shifts your attention away from problems and concerns. The end result can be a quick remedy for stress that is easily worked into the busiest of routines.

Getting Away from Noise

A fact of everyday modern life is that noise is all around us. If you're out of doors, chances are you will encounter a variety of sounds: the rumble of automobile traffic, mixing engine noise, blaring horns, and the occasional blast of a motorcycle or juiced-up car; the thunder of jet aircraft; radios blaring out of open car windows or from people carrying around portables; the clamor of a construction crew working on a new campus structure.

Go into a dorm or other building, and it may be an entirely different, but still noisy, environment. People are talking and laughing, and different brands of rock music seem to be waging a contest for everyone's attention.

When it comes to stress, noise can be a real problem. Various studies have shown a link between high levels of noise and both physical and psychological problems. What often happens is that too much noise wears on the body and becomes a stressor, eventually producing the same kinds of results as other causes of stress.

On the college scene, noise can be more of a problem than you might realize. Those glossy brochures and other materials may show the campus to be a quiet place perfect for pursuing your studies, but in the real world things are often quite different.

Sure, libraries are usually the quiet refuges they have always been, and classrooms are generally peaceful enough. But what about the place you have to live? Dormitories and apartments can be among the noisiest of places. Television sets, tape players, radios, typewriters, computer printers, electric hairdryers, and dozens of other sources of noise can add to the clamor.

150

Much depends on the roommate. What happens if yours always insists on playing the radio at all hours of the day or night, but you're the type who prefers to turn it off when studying? Or what if you feel the same way about playing music all the time, but your tastes in music are entirely different? In cases such as these, one student's entertainment becomes another's irritating noise.

You can't escape from noise entirely, but try to grab some quiet time every day if possible. "Everyone needs to get away from noise and experience some quiet time," says Nancy Slater of Columbia College in Missouri. "Some colleges have quiet rooms just for this purpose, and you can always take advantage of the library. Or go take a walk in the woods. Do whatever is necessary to get away from noise on a regular basis."

CHAPTER 12

*A*VOIDING STRESSFUL FINANCIAL PROBLEMS

*M*uch of the stress people face today is relatively new in the human experience. For ancient peoples, the fight-or-flight situation described in chapter 2 was a literal choice between fighting a fierce animal, or perhaps an equally deadly human, and running away. But today, stress is more likely to be induced by something prehistoric people never heard of.

One of these stressors is money—or more precisely, the lack of it. Problems related to finances rank among the most common sources of stress for all kinds of people. College students, unfortunately, are not immune to financial pressures. In fact, college is where many young men and women first learn to deal with money and first encounter the difficulties that inevitably arise when financial obligations equal or exceed monetary resources.

At first glance this may seem nothing new, especially if your family encountered any financial difficulties while you were growing up. But then it was largely someone else's worry. Now, as an adult trying to negotiate new responsibilities and a new level of independence, money matters may provide some of your most difficult problems.

"Money is one of the leading reasons students drop out of school," says Larry David, vice president of College Survival, Inc. "Financial pressures can be a real problem for college students."

The good news, though, is that problems related to money can be avoided or surmounted. By thinking in financial terms and developing certain basic skills, you can limit stress caused by financial considerations.

Developing a Budget

Unless you have been unusually independent, you probably have never had to develop a budget or do what's even harder—stick to one. Sure, your family probably has some kind of budget, even if very informally structured. And as a member of the family, you've had to live within the financial realities of your family's particular situation.

As a college student, though, you suddenly move from the position of consumer to manager. Ready or not, you may find yourself in a new, unfamiliar situation where parents are no longer around to handle daily expenses, and your own ability to take care of the financial end of things may be tested for the first time.

What comes as something of a shock to many students is the way money seems to disappear. Where did it all go? How will I make it to the end of the semester or maybe even the end of the month? Why is everything so expensive, anyway?

An effective means of dealing with all this is to develop a budget. Budgeting is often complicated, but it doesn't have to be that way. Don't think of a budget as some kind of rigid structure requiring a pile of detailed facts and figures, and many hours of attention. With a full load of classes, who would have time for this anyway? Instead, think of a budget as a highly personalized, general road map for helping you manage your money. After all, you certainly don't want to spend more money than you have. Just think of the prospect of running out of funds several weeks before the semester is over—it's not an attractive idea. With a simple budget plan, you can avoid such problems.

The first step in budgeting as a student is simply writing down all your financial obligations in one column and then your funds or income that will cover those obligations in another. There are many variations of this, and you can consult a business textbook or family planning guide for samples. The main point is to plan very carefully the way you will spend your money over the course of an academic year, preferably listed on a monthly basis.

Once you have developed a written budget plan, consult it frequently, and stick to it! That's the hard part, but unless you have someone who will bail you out if you become overextended, following your budget is a must.

Building Basic Skills in Handling Money

In addition to learning to budget, you should master other basic skills in dealing with money. For example, do you know how to handle a checking account? If not, this is a skill you should develop as soon as possible. It's not really that complicated, and you can learn the basics with a minimum of effort. You don't need much money to open an account and become familiar with the logistics of depositing funds, writing checks, and balancing your checkbook. In fact, doing this while still in high school can be a smart move just to become accustomed to the process.

Why bother with a checking account? That saves you the risk of carrying too much cash around which can be lost or stolen, and goes hand in hand with good budgeting because checks provide a record of your spending. In addition, a canceled check will count as proof that you paid for something—whether it's tuition or a pair of jeans—long after you have lost or discarded the receipt. And that can prove invaluable if there is ever a mistake that calls into question whether you actually made a payment.

In managing a checking account, be sure to take caution in dealing with automatic teller machines. Many banks have these units installed right on college campuses, and they can be convenient when you need some cash after normal banking hours or when you don't have time to go to the bank. But they can also provide a fast track to financial problems. Because it's so easy to withdraw money (all you do is insert a card, punch in a few numbers, and grab some cash), you can overspend almost before you know it.

If you utilize these machines, make sure you record each transaction promptly. Don't just cram the receipt into a purse or wallet, or overall withdrawals might accumulate to a substantial amount before you realize the commitments are larger than you had intended.

In addition, try not to visit automatic tellers—or the bank in general—too often. The less frequently you have access to cash, the less likely you are to spend it. And when you do make withdrawals, take out small amounts and try to make them last. Get in the habit of withdrawing $10 instead of $40 each time, and chances are you will waste less money.

Cutting College Costs

One half of the financial equation is assets. The amount of money you have (or can obtain) is one factor over which you may or may not have much control. The other half is outlay—how much you spend. This is something you *can* control, at least to some degree. You can't talk your college into lowering its tuition rates, of course. But if you think like a consumer and look for ways to cut costs, you can avoid paying any more than is necessary. And by saving on costs where possible, you can avoid financial strains and the stress that can accompany them.

For example, with a little foresight you can save on the costs of books, supplies, and other incidentals. If you haven't yet had your first encounter with the college bookstore, you may be in for an unpleasant surprise. Sure, books and supplies represent small-scale costs when compared with the high cost of tuition and fees. But because of those very fees, there may be precious little funds left over for books. Yet many textbooks cost as much as $30 apiece, and some are even more. At the same time, some professors require you to buy several different texts, with the end result being a hefty book bill every semester.

One easy way to reduce book expenses is simply buying used textbooks instead of new ones. College bookstores and private bookstores catering to students frequently sell second-hand books, sometimes on the same shelves as more expensive new versions. As long as the book represents the same edition, the used book will serve just fine. In fact, you can feel less restricted in underlining or making notes directly in the book, if that's your style.

You can also obtain used books from other students, usually at cheaper prices than can be found in bookstores. To locate them, ask other students, check out bulletin boards, or watch for ads in the college newspaper or local papers.

Another possibility is sharing books with a fellow student. By pooling resources in purchasing and using textbooks, you can reduce book expenditures substantially. This will not work for everyone, but for roommates or close friends who know each other to be reliable, it can be effective, especially with reference books or optional texts that you do not need to use every day. And in some courses, you can use library copies instead of buying every book covered. For example, an English literature course might cover several novels in addition to other material. Instead of buying every novel, you might read library versions of at least some of them.

You can also try to save money on typing paper, notebooks, pens, computer supplies, and other items by shopping at discount stores. Through comparison shopping and stockpiling of supplies, you can avoid the high prices common in college bookstores. On-campus stores may be convenient, but you can usually beat their prices. And no matter where you shop, take advantage of sales whenever possible.

You can save larger sums of money through creative scheduling and an awareness of the pricing that forms the basis for how your tuition and fees are calculated. This is an especially promising option if you attend a private college or one of the more expensive public institutions.

For example, you can realize substantial savings by enrolling for a few courses at a college offering a lower tuition rate and then transferring the credits back to your home institution. If a three-credit course costs $600 at your college but only $80 at a nearby community college, you can enroll in the cheaper course, earn your grade, and then transfer it back. As long as you obtain approval in advance (and most colleges will allow a reasonable number of transfer credits), you can "beat the system" in this way and save hundreds of dollars in the process.

You can accomplish the same thing by completing correspondence courses or by enrolling as a transient student during the summer at an inexpensive college near your home. Or you can earn credit for courses by passing standardized examinations, instead of actually enrolling. This will probably involve a reasonable testing fee, but not the tuition normally charged for the course.

Of course, with all these suggestions it is assumed that you have already selected or enrolled in a college. If you have not yet taken this step, you might want to consider the most effective method of all for saving college dollars: enrolling in an inexpensive two-year college and then transferring to a four-year college if you opt for a bachelor's degree. Many students save thousands of dollars by taking this approach.

Another strategy is cutting back on costs for room and board. Unless you commute from your home, a big part of your educational expenses will go toward housing and food. As with other expenses, you can pay whatever costs develop no matter how expensive, or you can save money by comparing costs and spending reasonably.

As a first step, take a close look at dormitory expenses compared with apartment living. Enterprising students often save substantial amounts by combining their resources and renting an off-campus apartment. If several students room together and split the cost of rent and utilities, the cost per person can be less than in a dormitory. Of course, this all depends on avoiding high-rent districts and finding good roommates, but in the right circumstances it can be a smart alternative.

No matter where you live, you can save on food expenses. Try fixing some of your own meals instead of relying entirely on the college cafeteria or on restaurants, and you can stretch your food budget.

You will have plenty to worry about in college without adding financial woes to the list. Just try to be a smart consumer and avoid wasting resources, and you will not only save money but also avoid undue stress related to your financial situation.

CHAPTER *13*

STRESS AND THE COMMUTING STUDENT

Most of the material covered in previous chapters applies to virtually all college students. Whether you go away to school or stay at home and commute to a nearby campus, you will face the same kinds of problems, ranging from test anxiety to the need for effective time management.

In a few key areas, however, the routine followed by commuting students may differ markedly from that faced by residential students. Those who choose to stay home certainly don't have to deal with homesickness, nor will they find themselves having to get along with a new roommate. And in most cases there will not be such an abrupt transition to the relative independence of life without parents around.

A number of other advantages also come into play. Commuting students avoid some of the huge expenses faced by other students. Not only are room-and-board costs eliminated, but tuition and fees might be much less at a local school, especially if it is a two-year college. Even if you eventually plan to earn a bachelor's degree, you can still reduce your total costs by nearly half by playing the role of transfer student. Taking advantage of the low tuition, you simply complete the first couple of years as a commuting student, earn the same basic credits as you would during the freshman and sophomore years elsewhere, and then transfer with full junior status at a senior institution.

Or you can complete a one- or two-year program designed to prepare you for a job rather than transferring. Associate degree (two-year) programs provide the alternative of attending only two years of college and then beginning a career in fields such as computer programming, nursing, engineering technology, drafting, respiratory therapy, secretarial science, and many others.

Going to a local two-year school or inexpensive four-year college can also limit potential problems in that in some ways, this involves less of a risk than going away to school. If you're not certain you even want to attend college, or wonder if you can make it academically, you can try out college life without risking so much money. And if you decide college is not for you, there will probably be less trauma in dropping out than if your family makes a big production of your going away, only to have you come back again as something less than a conquering hero.

You can also avoid the stress of heavy academic loads if you prefer to attend part-time, perhaps combining work with attending college. Such an option would probably be impractical when going away to school, for you would have too much time and money invested to justify attending college as anything but a full-time student.

On the other hand, the life of a commuting student offers its own particular stressors. As with any other decision, opting to commute represents something of a trade-off.

"For some students, commuting may not be all that

stressful," says Dr. Robert Stokes, director of continuing education at Villanova University in Philadelphia, Pennsylvania. "But for others, playing the commuting student's role brings its own unique sources of stress. Just driving a half hour to school, fighting to find a parking place and hustling to make it to class on time can be highly stressful, not to mention facing the challenges of trying to balance school and home life."

Handling the special situation of commuting to college requires the ability to stake out your role as a college student and fulfill it against other competing interests. Here are four basic tips for avoiding stress as a commuting student.

1. *Make it clear that going to college is Job 1.* Ford Motors has made the slogan "Quality is Job 1" famous, but you can adapt this motto and make it your own. Even if you work while attending school, make certain your family and friends realize that your number one priority is making it in college.

One of the major challenges commuting students encounter is simply finding space in their lives to take care of the academic work involved in going to college. Because you're still around the house, parents and friends may overlook your need to devote many hours to your studies. Instead, they may expect too much of you in terms of household chores or just plain socializing.

This can be an even bigger problem for adult students who have spouses and children of their own. With all the demands of normal family life, the role of college student can be pushed into the background.

According to Dr. Stokes, you should discuss this issue with family members and develop some guidelines about what each of you should expect out of the experience. "Talk with parents or other family members and let them know you will need study time," he advises. "And then make certain everyone continues to realize how important your college efforts are to you."

2. *Don't work too many hours.* It's not enough to gain the right support from family members. You must also place college work above any job you might have. Many commuting students hold down jobs, often out of genuine economic need. But even at that, you will be shorting yourself if you put in too many hours on the job.

"Commuting students often put impossible demands on themselves," says Dr. Joseph McCadden, an English instructor at Burlington County College in New Jersey. "Many have highly stressful jobs working in fast food restaurants or retail stores, and then they attempt full-time academic work. Too often by the end of the semester, they are in academic trouble."

If you must be employed, try to keep the number of hours you work every week to a minimum. Make do with less money if you have to, but don't allow a dead-end job to reduce your ability to perform well in college.

3. *Find a quiet place to study.* If possible, designate a special place in your home where you can pursue your studies in relative peace and quiet. This can be a bedroom, den, room in the basement, or whatever. The main factors are lack of noise and being sufficiently out of the way that you can avoid being interrupted all the time while you're trying to work.

If you can't achieve this at home, set up a regular pattern of studying in the college library or a public library near your home. In any case, make certain you have a place where you can "escape" the rest of the world while completing your academic work.

4. *Get involved on campus.* Just because you don't live on campus, that does not mean you can't participate in campus activities. There should be more to college than driving to school, attending classes, and driving back home or to work.

If you attend a community college, activities will be planned and scheduled with the particular needs of commuting students in mind. And even if you attend a school that caters primarily to residential students, many activities such as those described in chapter 5 will be open to you. Participating in just one club or organization will add spice to your college life and help reduce some of the stress caused by concentrating solely on academics.

CHAPTER 14

*W*INNING THE STRESS GAME

Keeping Things in Perspective

College can be great. It can make a big difference in your chances for a successful future. There is probably no better way to invest a few years of your life than by seeking a college degree.

It can also be fun. College forms the starting point for many enduring friendships and frequently even for marriages. Many older adults look back on their college days as the best times of their lives, and the same may be true for you someday.

Because we expect so much from college, it can be devastating if things don't work out. As pointed out previously, our own expectations and those of many others may be on the line, and a lack of apparent success can disappoint entire families, not to mention individuals.

A key factor to keep in mind, though, is that college is not an instant ticket to success. You can do great in college and still mess up your life. Or you can do poorly and still survive the situation.

It's important to keep things in perspective as you tackle the collegiate obstacle course. Doing your best is important, but don't expect yourself to be perfect. In the first place, you're bound to fail. No one else is flawless, and you're not going to be the twentieth century's first perfect student! Striving for perfection may sound like an admirable trait, but in the real world it almost certainly will lead to stress problems.

Does this mean you should forget about lofty goals? No, not at all. Ambition is fine, and as others have told you it would be a shame for you to waste your own special talents. By all means, do everything you can to live up to your potential.

But don't expect *too* much of yourself. Be realistic in expectations, especially in terms of performance that is competitive such as grades, athletic success, and award competitions. Work hard, try hard, and don't give up on yourself, but also give yourself a break sometimes.

Getting Professional Help

This book is intended to give you some commonsense, no-nonsense help with identifying stressful elements of the collegiate experience and in coping with them so that you can succeed in your college goals. It is *not* designed as a source of all the possible answers to everybody's particular stress-related problems.

The following point can't be emphasized too much. *If you begin to feel completely overwhelmed by college or by life in general, get some professional help.* This may mean simply talking to a counselor at your college, or it might mean consulting a physician, psychologist, or other health care professional. Whatever the case, don't be shy or reluctant to seek out help if you think you need it.

It might reassure you to know that college counselors follow a code of ethics that includes the duty to keep information confidential. You can go to them with the most private kind of information and rest assured that your privacy will be protected.

If you ever begin to experience suicidal thoughts, stop right there and get help! The problem of suicide is too important to be ignored—by the individual or by society at large. In September 1988, three New York college students committed suicide within a one-week period, and suicides are a too-frequent problem among students. One of every eight deaths of persons ages 15–24 is by suicide, according to *Statistical Abstracts of the United States*. More young people die at their own hands than from cancer, heart disease, diabetes, pneumonia, or any other cause except accidents. But any problem you might encounter in college is *not* worth dying for! If such thoughts ever enter your mind, get help immediately.

Making a Go of It

All things considered, college represents one of the most enormous challenges of your life. No matter what institution you attend or major you pursue, there are bound to be times when stress becomes a problem.

But hang in there! Stress can be managed, and college can be survived. Try to play it smart in dealing with the pressures of college life, and you will be fine.

"Remember, you're not the only one encountering this situation," says Kyle Morgan of Ohio State University. "Just take advantage of the resources available to you, and you can cope with the stress of the college experience."

INDEX

Other Books of Interest from the College Board

dren to explore careers and find alternatives suited to their interests and abilities. ISBN: 0-87447-305-5, $12.95

002482 *How to Pay for Your Children's College Education,* by Gerald Krefetz. Practical advice to help parents of high school students, as well as of young children, finance their children's college education. ISBN: 0-87447-248-2, $12.95

003373 *Index of Majors, 1989-90.* Lists over 500 majors at the 3,000 colleges and graduate institutions, state by state, that offer them. ISBN: 0-87447-337-3, $14.95 (Updated annually)

002911 *Profiles in Achievement,* by Charles M. Holloway. Traces the careers of eight outstanding men and women who used education as the key to later success. (Hardcover, ISBN: 0-87447-291-1, $15.95); 002857 paperback (ISBN: 0-87447-285-7, $9.95)

002598 *Succeed with Math,* by Sheila Tobias. A *practical* guide that helps students overcome math anxiety and gives them the tools for mastering the subject in high school and college courses as well as the world of work. ISBN: 0-87447-259-8, $12.95

003225 *Summer on Campus,* by Shirley Levin. A comprehensive guide to more than 250 summer programs at over 150 universities. ISBN: 0-87447-322-5, $9.95

003039 *10 SATs: Third Edition.* Ten actual, recently administered SATs plus the full text of *Taking the SAT,* the College Board's official advice. ISBN: 0-87447-303-9, $9.95

002571 *Writing Your College Application Essay,* by Sarah Myers McGinty. An informative and reassuring book that helps students write distinctive application essays and explains what colleges are looking for in these essays. ISBN: 0-87447-257-1, $9.95

002474 *Your College Application,* by Scott Gelband, Catherine Kubale, and Eric Schorr. A step-by-step guide to help students do their best on college applications. ISBN: 0-87447-247-4, $9.95

To order by direct mail any books not available in your local bookstore, please specify the item number and send your request with a check made payable to the College Board for the full amount to: College Board Publications, Department M53, Box 886, New York, New York 10101-0886. Allow 30 days for delivery. An institutional purchase order is required in order to be billed, and postage will be charged on all billed orders. Telephone orders are not accepted, but information regarding any of the above titles is available by calling Publications Customer Service at (212) 713-8165.